Help Your Kids Become

# Millionaires

By Larry Lynch,

Executive Director of EES, Inc.

ISBN 0-7414-2538-6



***Published by:***

INFINITY
PUBLISHING.COM

***1094 New DeHaven Street, Suite 100***
***West Conshohocken, PA 19428-2713***
***Info@buybooksontheweb.com***
***www.buybooksontheweb.com***
***Toll-free (877) BUY BOOK***
***Local Phone (610) 941-9999***
***Fax (610) 941-9959***

***Printed in the United States of America***

***Printed on Recycled Paper***

***Published July 2005***

# Table of Contents

# Foreword

My dad was a high school math teacher. He was frugal with his schoolteacher salary, and I was encouraged to get a job, save my money, and pay my debts. So I shoveled snow, picked apples, weeded the garden, and worked as a busboy, construction laborer, and more. After high school, I worked in a gas station for a year before I went to college. Throughout college, there were many different jobs, including playing Santa Claus during the holidays and cleaning a hospital kitchen on the overnight shift. My eventual degree in sociology had no direct relationship to my growing collection of job experiences. Some jobs were better than others; the best full-time job I ever had was as a motorcycle mechanic, even though I was laid off every fall and lived on unemployment compensation through the winter.

After many years, I ended up with stock from technology companies I had worked for, and saved the stock because it was just like money, and Dad had taught me to save my money. It was also important that I thought that the companies I worked for were responsible, with honest professionals and products that offered significant value. After years of doing nothing, the stocks soared during the dot-com bubble, and I sold at the right time. Dad had taught me to pay my debts, so I did that, left my sales job, and got myself a really nice car.

$$$$$

Early one beautiful summer Sunday morning, I drove to the local convenience store to get some newspapers. There was a line. The guy in front of me was wearing a house painter's smock. His shoes were mostly covered with wet paint. He had already done a half day's work at 9 a.m. on a Sunday. When he got to the counter, he purchased a two-foot-long strip of lottery scratch tickets. He went down them one by one, getting madder and madder as he had no winners. In disgust, he threw the losing tickets in the direction of a trash container and stomped out of the store.

He had just lost a morning's work on lottery tickets. He was big and he was mad, and I did not think he would have been interested in a discussion on probability (Dad was a MATH teacher) or on saving or investing. But what had happened was wrong. He had been at work as soon as the sun was up and now he had nothing to show for it. If someone had just gotten to him when he was a kid and said....

I had connections at the local schools. Maybe I could get to his kids and help them avoid making the same mistake.

$$$$$

That was the start of Education for Economic Security, Inc., a nonprofit organization that teaches financial education to Middle School students in a number of towns near where I live and the painter paints. The name of our program is, So Who Wants to Be a Millionaire? Over the years, as this project has grown, I was able to research more and more about macro and personal finance, and learn about teaching kids.

Much of what I learned from research was disheartening. The American dream of upward mobility seems now to be mostly a dream. The division between the absurdly rich and the rest of us is growing wider. Credit card debt is the most frequent cause of kids dropping out of college.

However, some things are positive and exciting. The kids of today are obviously going to live longer and healthier lives. Many intelligent people want to make the world a better place, and there are tremendously powerful new personal financial tools that can be used by everyone. If you research the financial tools, understand how they work, and do the math (remember my dad, the math teacher...), real economic security can be created for 90 percent or more of all Americans in one or two generations. Having a million or more tax-free dollars after fifty years of work can provide very good economic security.

$$$$$

This is America, a country with unique ways of doing things. Here, the financial future of individuals is not controlled by the government; instead, powerful financial tools are available to individuals for their own use. Here, individuals can secure a comfortable future for themselves, but they need to take "ownership" of their financial well-being to make things happen.

Fifty years ago there were organizations that provided the individual with financial security. Many people worked most of their lives for a single company, and that company, or the union that represented them to that company, provided a defined benefit pension. Defined benefit means that you know what you are going to get, usually for the rest of your life. Today, this has all changed, and the responsibility for taking care of your children as they age is yours and theirs.

Today, large, established organizations like United Airlines, Bethlehem Steel, General Motors and even the Catholic Church are facing major problems with their pension plans. Although there is federal support for company pension plans (through the Pension Benefit Guarantee Corporation) , the financial structure of that guarantee is questionable[1]. Most companies that offer funding for retirement have moved to 401(k) plans where their commitment is only to making a contribution to the plan. And that is the good news. Many companies are now offering only to administer a 401(k) only; the company makes NO contributions to the plan, all contributions to the plan are the responsibility of the individual only! Many of these plans are also "self directed," so the responsibility for investing those funds falls back on the individual.

Job patterns have also changed dramatically and many people will work at many different jobs throughout their life. The only way to make sense of a "retirement" program is to put it in the hands of either the state or the individual. In America, most of the responsibility is passed to the individual.

There is a secure financial future available to almost all Americans, but it will not just happen. The most important first step everyone must take towards financial security is to accept responsibility for it. Begin with the right attitude, educate yourself, and act. These are three steps lead to financial security. Each of us must begin with the right attitude; each of us must learn about the financial tools available to us, and each of us must act. It is, perhaps, easier to create a welfare state than for everyone of us to take these steps, but the benefits of having the individual taking responsibility are obvious. We get personal financial security, and we create stronger, more self-reliant citizens.

$$$$$

So, we have a new plan and a new message. There are powerful financial tools, which did not exist ten years ago, that make the dream of becoming a millionaire an obtainable reality.

There is a new opportunity for economic security based not on government programs, not on the charity of others, and not on luck, but based on the laws of mathematics. We want everyone to get rich. Everyone means the people with credit card debts of $25,000 as well as those who can't even qualify for their first credit card.

$$$$$

Many people helped make this book happen. Here are people who have taken action to make the future more secure for us all:

- "Mike" Csikszentmihalyi, a sociology teacher at Lake Forest College many years ago who inspired me to find tools for constructive social change.

- Joe Sawyer, principal of the Floral Street Elementary School in Shrewsbury, Massachusetts, who encouraged and assisted me in making the first Millionaire financial education program.

- Donna Cox, chairperson of the Corridor Nine Chamber of Commerce School/Business Committee, who pushed me to grow the Millionaire program.

- Joe MacDonough of Westborough Bank, who supported our Millionaire program from the very first day.

- Karyn Polito, the Massachusetts state representative (R) who provided personal and political support.

- My wife, Chris Nevin, and our daughters who wondered why Dad was working on his computer at 6 a.m.

Thanks also to the multiple financial professionals who have assisted and/or volunteered their time to teach financial education. They see the wealth that can be created with an appropriate attitude toward the future and with planning, and they also have seen see the disasters when plans are not made.

| | |
|---|---|
| Greg Mangan | Metro West Financial Partners |
| Kim Corwin | NewLeaf Financial |
| Christopher Rowe | Tycoon Research |

| | |
|---|---|
| Tim Higgins | AmEx Financial |
| Robin Morrell & Lew Simmons | Merrill Lynch |
| Bill Dion | PFC |
| Scott MacCausland | LPL Financial |
| Multiple individuals at | Fidelity Investments |

I thank all the afore mentioned individuals for their time, effort, support, and counsel. It was because of them that the *So Who Wants to Be a Millionaire?* financial education program for middle school students is working. The results of our research for that program inspired this book.

This book is dedicated to the person who started it all: my dad, the math teacher,

**Ransom Van Brunt Lynch**

[1] Robert D. Reischauer, Director, Congressional Budget Office before the Oversight Committee on Ways and Means, U.S. House of Representatives. August 11, 1992.

# Chapter 1: You CAN Do This

Our promise to you is that, if your child can gain and keep a job appropriate for his or her age, he or she can become a millionaire or even a multimillionaire. We can make your children wealthy for half of their adult life, and improve your own financial situation at the same time. Our promise is based on these assumptions:

- Your children have opportunities and financial tools that you never had.
- The financial tools are easy, well-known, and legal
- The key to our plan is to develop an appropriate attitude toward money.
- You will have to work to make this happen.
- You may need to make choices that are hard at first, but will be painless after a few months.
- You will need to follow through on the choices you make, and that won't be easy at the start.
- You have powerful forces working against you.

Everyone has a different family and financial environment. We will point out the issues that need to be addressed and trust that you will find a way to make it happen. If you want to change your children's financial future and your own, you must be prepared to make changes in the way you handle finances. The plan in this book is real and it works.

It is aimed at families with incomes of $25,000 to $250,000 per year. If you would like to be rich without making any changes, we suggest you find a lucky rabbit's foot, and we hope you find this book entertaining. If you expect to gain true wealth instantly, we suggest you look for the same rabbit's foot. If you are prepared to make some changes in your life and build serious wealth for yourself and for your children, this book is a road map and you are the driver.

You may want many things for your children:

- a health plan to protect their health
- a big wedding with hundreds of people (very important in some cultures)
- vacations so that the whole family can go off and have fun together (our personal favorite)
- a college education
- braces for their teeth
- a home in a suburb where there are good schools

To get these things, we hope you are saving money or are planning to save. However, most of us have limits to how much we can save, and we cannot save everything we earn. We have to make choices. Making intelligent choices is one of the key parts of being both an adult and a parent. This book is going to offer you one additional thing to save for. It sounds a bit radical, but don't simply dismiss it as ridiculous until you have heard our reasoning.

Your parents and their parents would laugh at this. But you are living in a different age, and your children will be living in an even more different age. Your children's financial needs will not be the same as your needs or your parents' needs or their parents' needs. We want you to start saving for your children's retirement—now. That is correct: start now to save for their retirement. They are going to need your help, and it is much more important than you think. No, we do not think your savings alone will provide a million dollars. However, if you follow our plan and can make an early financial contribution to your children's future, they can be wealthy for the second half of their adult lives. Modest contributions by you now can make a huge financial impact at a time in your children's lives when they may really need some help. You need to make them rich, because they will have major financial issues that you will not have and that your parents could not have imagined. With your help, your children can be millionaires and more. You have the capability of making them wealthy for half of their adult life, even if you and they have little now.

Your financial situation is unique. You may think that the numbers are out of line in the examples we give. Don't worry about the numbers; learn the principle behind the numbers. A million dollars may sound like a lot of money to you, but we are talking about fifty years from now, and by then it will be worth a lot less than it is today. It is, however, a good, round number. Once you understand the plan and begin the process, it will be easy to make adjustments to meet your goals. If your family is living comfortably in a low-cost part of the country and have managed your finances well, an income of $3,000 per month may seem to be extravagant. But if you live in Manhattan or in San Francisco, $3,000 per month may not be enough to pay for your parking spaces.

If you are in a low cost-of-living area, you are likely to find that your income is also lower. The amount you and your children can save will then be lower. The good news is that your financial needs will be lower. Still, your children's financial needs in the second half of their adult life will be great, no matter where they live.

As we will repeat multiple times: this book is a map, but you are the driver and you make the decisions.

## Chapter Summary

- Your children today have opportunities and financial tools that you never had.

- Attitude is the key element in shaping the financial future for your children.

- You and your children will need to make choices and take control of your and their financial behavior.

- If your child can, at an appropriate age, gain and keep a job, we will show you how your child can become a millionaire.

# Chapter 2:
# Your Kids Need Your Help

## Retirement History

In 1931, the average male life expectancy was fifty-seven. When Social Security was established by the Social Security Act of 1935, it was aimed at ensuring a minimum income for about five years, starting at age sixty-five, which was when people were expected to retire. Note that retirement happened years after the average life expectancy. Obviously, people were not expected to live long back in the 1930s, and it was correctly expected that

Social Security payments would average only a few years. That was then. In 2000, a worker who was sixty-five could expect to live another eighteen years. Payments from Social Security, assuming you have been paying into the system most of your life, will provide about enough to keep you just over the federal poverty income level. Hello! That would be eighteen years at poverty levels if you retire today at 65 with no other income plan.

## Retirement Is Gone

My father taught in the same school for forty-five years. The longest I ever worked for a single company was seven years. I have had four totally different careers. The children of today will live in a society with more rapid changes and more new opportunities than we can imagine. For most of us, what was once called "retirement" is simply gone. The expectation of a gold watch and a pension check must be replaced by a carefully thought out financial plan that is owned and managed by the individual. This plan will offer much more than "retirement"; it will offer your children real economic security, pride, respect and the opportunity to create a Greater Good in a community where they will feel at home.

As it was in the old days, so it is even today; once a certain age has been reached, a bureaucracy can force you from your job. You are pushed out the door and given a check. Unfortunately, this may not be the time at which you want to take that step. Too bad. According to the rules, at an arbitrary age, you are required to resign from your position and ...

In the future, the magic date of "retirement" will become very blurred. If you have real economic security, when working for someone no longer is attractive, you move on to something you would rather do. If you want to stay on at your old job, it is your choice. The power to decide is moving from the company policy to the individual. But the individual must have economic security to be able to take action. Economic security comes from having a lot of money "in the bank," and knowing how to handle it.

## The Good News/Bad News

It may be that you can expect an eighteen-year retirement today, but "retirement" will be very different for your children. It will be a LONG time before your children "retire." Think about the medical advances of the last fifty years. What will we see in the next fifty or sixty years? In the last fifty years, we have seen the average life expectancy increase about nine years. Let us be very conservative and say that we expect to add only another nine years of life expectancy over the next fifty years. Add those nine years to the eighteen non-earning year life expectancy of today and you get twenty-seven years. More than a quarter of a century. And that is a MINIMUM. That is a long time to live just over the poverty level, and it assumes the Social Security system is able to offer the same benefits as it does today.

This was not a problem that previous generations worried much about; they didn't live that long. It is likely to be an issue for you, and we hope that you are taking steps to be sure you are financially secure enough not to burden your children during the later part of your adult life. But the issue is critical for your children.

Putting simple, round numbers to the future of today's children, our plan is for about twenty years of growing up, forty years of income from jobs, and forty years of economic security that will let them have lots of attractive choices. Do you think your children would like to spend half of their adult life with serious wealth?

There is also the very real possibility that your children will see a dramatic, make that a really dramatic, rise in longevity. Advances being made today may extend the life of a person born today to well past 100 years, perhaps past 130 years or more. This would cause massive changes in every aspect of our society except one. The need for wealth in everyone's senior years will be even more critical. Bottom line: you need to help your children plan for their financial future, and start on it soon.

Political issues will greatly affect your child's financial future. The changing demographics of this country are challenging the financial well-being of Social Security, Medicare, and Medicaid. We hope that the skyrocketing national debt will be wiped out by another economic boom, but until that happens we have serious financial issues that will cost money to fix -- your money and your children's money. There are real financial challenges for us and for our children in the years ahead. The situation is clear: if you want to have some economic security for your children, you need to see that they are in control. You should not expect the government to make more than a trivial contribution to their financial future. The financial future of your children is in your and their hands. You need to find a plan and get it working soon!

Harvard University's Consumer Bankruptcy Project found that there has been a 213 percent increase in bankruptcy for individuals over sixty-five, as people live longer; meanwhile, pharmaceuticals and other medical expenses are rapidly increasing in cost.[1] We have a serious issue now, and it will get a lot worse before it gets better. You need to act now to protect your children.

## What Is Economic Security?

Economic security means knowing where the money you need to live comfortably will be coming from for the indefinite future. Bill Gates obviously has economic security. He is a very sharp guy with more money than anyone else. He spends much of his time trying to effectively use that money to make the world a better place. While some may admire him, most of us have more mundane issues to worry about like eating and creating a home.

In the simplest terms, economic security is having enough money so that you can be assured you will be able to live with reasonable comfort for the indefinite future.

Unfortunately, the amount of money you need for economic security is likely to be more, much more, than you have ever imagined.

There are two obvious programs that you might think offer financial security. The first is Social Security, which will not give you enough money no matter how thrifty you are. Social Security was never intended to be a full retirement program and will not be one in the future. While the checks will keep coming once you qualify and apply, it may be that you would like to gain economic security before Social Security starts sending you those tiny checks.

The second type of program is called an annuity, which is offered in many different forms by hundreds of insurance companies. It is a form of insurance: you give money to the insurance company and the company will pay it back to you over a period of time. That period of time can be as long as you live. The obvious point is that the amount of money you can get back from the insurance company is completely dependent on the amount you put in. Insurance companies, like most other companies, intend to make a profit. While most of their profit will be on the investment return they make on your money, they are not about to give you more than you have coming. You can assume a lifetime annuity might pay you as much as 4 percent per year of what you put in—depending on variables such as your age. So, if you put $100,000 into an annuity, you might be able to get an income of as much as $4,000 per year for life—not much money. Many annuities also have the disadvantage that they charge high fees.

There are other ways you may be able to use your savings and investments to create a flow of money, but if we are talking about economic security, you need to be sure you are going to get that money. Social Security and annuities don't require much action on your part. Should you wish to have greater return on your investment, you will need to learn a lot about investing, take some risks, and get some good advice (see Chapter 10).

Here are some additional considerations. The higher your lifestyle, the greater the financial needs will be before you can have economic security. If you are living on $40,000 per year, a sure income of $50,000 should look just great. But if you are used to a lifestyle of $100,000, that same sure income will look like a crisis.

Different parts of the country have different costs of living, and that can have a great impact on your feeling of economic security. It is about twice as expensive to live in San Jose, California, as it is to live in Las Cruces, New Mexico, or Jackson, Tennessee, or Albany, New York. But it is about 20 percent less expensive to live in San Jose, California, than in New York City.

Things do tend to average out so that the average person in San Jose, California, is bringing in about twice the income as the average person in Jackson, Tennessee. So, we would expect that the average person in San Jose would be able to save and invest about twice as much money.

Rocky Mount, North Carolina, is not far from the national average for a cost of living. An investment of $2,000 per year after fifty years of investing and compounding could generate an income of about $3,400 per month.[2] You may get an additional $1,000 per month from Social Security, starting at around seventy years of age. That supplies an income of over $50,000 per year in today's dollars and with very few taxes. In Rocky Mount, that could give most people a reasonable lifestyle, if their medical costs were covered.

You, however, are not an average person and you do not have an average cost of living or an average risk tolerance and your children do not have average lifestyle expectations. You are a unique individual. If you want a simple amount that will give you economic security, invest 5 percent of your income wisely every year from the time you are eighteen, shelter it from taxes, and you should be able to find comfortable economic security with lots of choices and options before you reach seventy.

It may be a bit late for you to start investing for yourself at age eighteen, and our Millionaire plan is based on the huge advantages of investing over time. Therefore, while it may be a good plan for you, it is a brilliant plan for your children, because the payoff will be huge for the next generation.

## Your Children Can be Millionaires

While we hope this book may assist you in improving your finances, this book is focused on your children's financial future and, to address that, we will spend time on childhood development and the creation and encouragement of the attitudes that will make your children wealthy. Our plan is to have you do two very different things at the same time and with the same goal.

**1) Put a financial program in place that will give your children a huge head start on serious wealth**

**2) Educate your children so they will be able to carry on the financial program you have started.**

You will only have about twenty years to get these things done and working, but if you do it well, you will see the results for many years after you have passed the financial torch on to your children.

Governments can change their mind and national financial situations change, so we will tell you about a "miracle" more powerful than the whims of the government that you can use to protect your children's wealth. It is called "compound interest." Albert Einstein called it the eighth wonder of the world.

*Heather and Nick Korman[3] are the parents of two girls, Natasha and Vera. Heather is a physical therapist and Nick sells cars and trucks. Heather's income is steady, currently at $60,000 per year, while Nick's income has been up and down over the years. They live in the expensive Northeast and own two older cars and a small house with a big mortgage.*

*Heather and Nick are aware of the impending financial crisis their kids will be facing and are also concerned about their own long-term future. But as Nick points out: "Here in America, you have the problem of people living too long. Back in Russia, where I came from, the average life expectancy is going DOWN. For many people there, life is worse under capitalism than it was under Communism, and it was pretty bad under Communism. A long life expectancy for my kids is a problem I am thrilled to be able to worry about!"*

## Chapter Summary

• Your children will face major financial problems in their later years, problems that your parents did not have.

• You can assume your children will spend decades in "retirement," much longer than you or your parents.

• Social Security was never intended to pay for the full cost of retirement; it is only a modest assistance.

• Even today, senior citizens are finding it very difficult to make ends meet.

• This book has several very specific plans that can make your children very wealthy and help your finances too!

[1] http://todaysseniorsnetwork.com/more_debt_problems.htm
[2] This assumes that the investors are knowledgeable or have skilled assistance, have earned 10 percent on their investments, and that inflation has averaged 3 percent. A sure investment like an annuity could reduce that amount by 10 to 25 percent
[3] Unless noted otherwise, we have changed the names of the characters used in this book or they are composite and fictional characters used to illustrate situations that people face every day.

# Chapter 3: Cons & Attitude

There are at least half a dozen organizations that want to sell you a program that can make millions in the Real Estate market. "Quit the Nine-to-Five job and get rich the easy way." The program typically tells you to find a person that wants to sell their property quickly at less than the market value. You buy the house using no-money-down financing (your credit) and sell it making a big profit. And on the TV ads you can see people that have actually made thousands of dollars following these programs. And if you saw it on TV, it must be true, right??

HOG WASH! Let's start with the obvious. How many people sell the largest single investment in their life for less than market value? And if they are that dumb, how did they get the house in the first place? Then what happens when the Real Estate market goes down, because you can be guaranteed that at some point, it will. And the success stories you see on TV? If you have 10,000 people a month getting the program for year after year, someone is going to have success. That is called luck! The TV ads, the seminars, all promise to make millions off the Real Estate. And even we agree that it is absolutely true. The millions are made by the people selling the programs! If their Real Estate plan was so great, why are they bothering to create, advertise and sell a teaching the program to others?

Our Millionaire program is very different. It is not a get-rich-quick scheme, it is a help your kids become smarter about money and give them a huge head start on wealth that will last them for half their lifetime. We also do not want you to quit your job. You now have the best job you can find and we hope you will be able to get a better one soon. Please don't give up a job because of what some TV show or book says. Take the hundreds or thousands of dollars those get-rich-quick programs want you to give to someone else and invest it in your family. If you follow our program, that money could amount to hundreds of thousands of dollars. We say "If it sounds too good to be true, it is probably too good to be true." And if you are broke, it is harder to make your kids rich. Keep your real job! Use the tools that the government and mathematics offers everyone and get rich! With our program you don't even need to make huge profits, but you need to avoid loosing money on get-rich-quick scams.

Avoiding big losses is even more important than making big gains. Just do the math. If you have $1000 invested and make a 50% profit, at the end of the year you have $1500. If you loose 50% the next year, at the end of that year you will only have $750, which is $250 less than you had at the start. Just to make it a little worse, you are likely to half to pay income taxes on that $500 profit you made. You must minimize losses.

We do not want you to take big risks. All the numbers in this book are based on making a 10% return on your investments, which is about average (see Chapter 11). You will hear of investments that offer much higher returns. If they offer high returns, they will have higher risks. If someone tells you that there are little or no risks involved, WATCH OUT!

The most important aspect of your children's life you need to influence to provide them economic security is their **ATTITUDE**. There are times in your child's life when it is difficult to influence attitude. Obviously, it is difficult, though not impossible, to make a great influence on attitude before your child can speak. Unfortunately, it is also frequently difficult, but again not impossible, to influence a child on many subjects after puberty starts, and suddenly he or she knows everything and, at the same time, knows that you know nothing.

Yes, there are financial tools we will show you, and legal points to understand, but none of these items will be worth more than a hill of beans unless we can shape your child's attitude.

Having the right attitude is more important than having money. Do you think we are crazy? Think about this. Many people who win lotteries in excess of $1 million have spent the money and are in worse financial shape five years after they win the money. Even worse, more than a few lottery winners end up in bankruptcy. The key is not the money, these "winners" were given the money, but the attitude. As a parent, you can influence your children's attitudes better than anyone else. If you would like a little wealth for yourself, you might consider changing your attitude about spending, saving, and investing money.

*Heather does not like dealing with finances. She is a hands-on person and does not enjoy dealing with analytical issues. On the other hand, in her job she sees lots of senior citizens who are having difficult financial times and wants to be sure this does not happen to her family. "Old people come in to get physical issues addressed and we show them exercises and work with them to extend their range of motion or whatever. But what is really going on for some is that these bills are being paid by Medicare, and just having someone to talk to and to have someone care for them is more important than the physical therapy. The event of the week may be coming to physical therapy. They are alone. They sit in their homes and watch TV and that is about all. Getting old like that sucks!"*

*She goes on: "But everyone is not in that situation; lots of old people are active as all get-out with church and family activities, hobbies, other friends, gardening, social activities, and even a vacation now and then. The real difference is money. I get to see both sides and I don't want the bad side to happen to me or my kids.*

*"If we had tons of money it wouldn't be a problem, but that is not us. We have to act now, and I'll learn whatever I have to if it will keep us financially Okay."*

Nick chimed in: *"The place that the financial future gets me nervous is in the supermarket. We are tight with our money and we shop a lot in the discount/warehouse places. I see old people with shopping lists that have dollars written down. They can't spend more than a fixed amount. Politicians talk about senior citizens having to choose between food and medicine. I can't tell what choices some old people are trying to make, but some of them find it obviously tough to make ends meet. I don't want my kids to be in that situation."*

To teach the right attitude, you need to show the right attitude. You need to show your children the difference between want and need. Yes, you may want another pair of shoes, but you may not need them. When you are shopping with your children, explain to them that you are making careful choices and you cannot and do not want to buy everything in the store.

In addition to attitude, you need to pay attention to details: You need to have your own house in order before you explain to a guest (or your child) how to keep his or her house in order. Do you have a budget? Do you have a long-term financial plan? How much is your credit card debt? While this book is aimed at building financial security for your children, you are not going to be able to get them to make the right moves unless they see you doing those same things yourself.

# Chapter 4: Walk the Walk

You are looking for change, right? You want to make a change in your children's financial future. You are also the person in charge. So if you really want change, you are going to have to change your own behavior. If you don't make a change, then your financial future is not likely to change.

What we need to focus on is your credibility with your children. We want you to "talk the talk" (teach them the steps they need to take) but if you want them to believe you, you also must "walk the walk" (show them the steps they need to take). Your next steps are:

- Developing Financial Discipline
- Managing your Debt
- Restricting Use of Credit Cards
- Spending and Saving Wisely
- Budgeting
- Planning your Financial Future
- Making Family Finances Transparent

## Discipline

Everyone approaches life with different attitudes toward structure. Some people like a structured environment with plans and rules; some prefer to operate more organically, as "free spirits". To make any financial program work, you will need to have some discipline, do some planning, and make yourself some rules that you will actually follow. If this is not something that has "fit" your lifestyle in the past, consider this a great opportunity to learn and grow. We want to put you in control of your financial life and future, and thereby the financial future of your children. While many things will affect your life, the final responsibility for what you make of your life is yours.

This means that, while you may like to have a credit card in your pocket and may want to buy whatever you see in the store -- don't do it. Again, it is all about attitude. This may be hard to do. We are counting on you to show your children that they can control their financial future. If you can learn to accept the responsibility for and exercise real control over your financial future, we can add wealth to your life and substantial wealth to the lives of your children.

## Debt

If you and your children are going to be wealthy, you need to be very careful about debt. Debt is a helpful, useful, and powerful financial tool. It is also dangerous.

Let us start with the very simple example that some people have yet to understand. You have an average of $500 of discretionary income each month — that is, money you can spend after you have paid your bills and living expenses. Each month, you have the opportunity to give that money to other people — that is, to buy things. If you spend $500, you will have another $500 the next month. If, in a single month, you spend $1,000 for stuff, you will need to borrow the extra $500 and you will have to pay for that debt. If you use a credit card to borrow the money, that $500 loan from the credit card company may cost you much, much more than $500. This means you will have less of your money in the future and someone else will have more of your money. You will now be working for the benefit of someone else. If you borrow money now, you will have less money in the future. If you invest money now, you are likely to have more money in the future. If you would like to be rich in the future, be extremely careful about debt today.

However, debt also can be a positive financial tool. Consider this example: Jean and Dan borrow $200,000 to buy a $240,000 house. At the end of ten years, they sell the house for $540,000. At a 10 percent mortgage rate, Jean and Dan will have already spent $192,493 in interest ($1,604 per month) and received a tax deduction for ten years. They will still owe $181,876 on their first mortgage, but show a profit of $318,124. That is a lot of profit! They could not have made that much profit unless they went into debt to buy the house in the first place. However, they were taking a risk. Sometimes, house values go down, and you may have paid more for a house than you can recover selling the house. This is local investing, where you can actually see your investment. However, just because you can see it, don't think that market forces totally out of your control can't dictate the value and profit from that investment (see Chapter 9).

Like most useful and powerful tools (cars, hammers,

factories, ladders, etc.) debt is both useful and dangerous. Every year millions of people in this country find themselves in serious trouble because they have more debt than they can afford. Credit card debt is perhaps the most dangerous. A budget can help you avoid excessive debt, understand how much your debt actually costs, and plan for the future.

In the example above with Jean and Dan buying and selling a house, let us make some suggestions as to the next steps they could take toward gaining economic security. The profit—$318,124—is a lot of money, but it is not enough for economic security. You need to live some place, so the typical next step is to take the profits from the first house and buy the next house. You want a bigger, nicer house, because this is America and everyone wants a bigger, fancier house. Unfortunately, when the value of your house went up, it is likely that the value of houses where you want to live also went up. Our suggestion is to spend only what you were paid for your old house on your new house, not one penny more. Do not go into debt. Remember the amount you paid in interest on your first house ($192,493)? That money is gone. But if you have no debt on the new house, you will not have to pay interest in the future -- which would be like saving $190,000. Hello! Anyone interested in $190,000 of savings??? Want to make that a bigger number? Good investing could make that $500,000 in ten years.

Let's look at it from a longer term perspective. How many times in your life will you have the opportunity to make $190,000 profit in a single transaction? It will not happen every day. When you are given the opportunity to have a lot of money, you need to take it. If you spend all that money and take on another big debt load, you have just given that money to someone else. Eliminating debt is a good step to gaining wealth. During your lifetime, there is a limited amount of money you will have. By eliminating debt, you get to keep more of that money.

If you want to give money to others, consider giving to a religious or charitable organization. It is likely to do greater good there than it would buying a status symbol or paying the interest on a debt for something you really don't need.

## Credit Cards

Debt in general is powerful, useful and dangerous. The most dangerous form of credit is the credit card. One of the major growth industries in America is credit card debt counseling. "The credit card industry is the most profitable one in the United States with annual earnings in the $30 billion range," according to BCS Alliance. "Many people might be surprised to learn that a single credit card issuer—MBNA—earned 1.5 times more profit than McDonald's in 2004. Citibank, another major credit card issuer, earns more profit than both Microsoft and Wal-Mart."[1]

That profit comes from people who work hard for their money and are now sending that hard-earned money to the credit card companies, because they just did not know financial basics. Using credit cards correctly is critical to your financial future. Here are some simple rules:[2]

- Never use a credit card to buy something you do not have the money (cash or savings) to pay for.

- Always pay the full amount of your credit card bill and don't be late.

- If you owe money on a credit card (you have not paid the bill in full and are now paying the typically outrageously high interest rates), do NOT use that card until you have paid that debt in full.

- Having fewer credit cards is better than having many. Having too many credit cards can damage your credit rating and will tempt you to do the shell game of using one credit card to pay another credit card, which can have you heading toward bankruptcy quickly.

- If you owe money to a credit card company, write down the amount of debt and put it in a prominent place in your kitchen. As the amount of your debt changes, change the number. Make that number go down and disappear!

If following these rules forces you to change your spending habits, consider this a great success. You will have taken a major step toward a better financial future.

If you have a credit card problem, there is a simple solution: Stop using credit cards. Although you may feel like destroying them, we suggest that you keep at least one. At some point, an emergency may arise, when having instant credit will be important, and a credit card can help. But unless it is a real emergency, do not use it!

Next, go to your local financial institution and get a debit card. To do this, you will need to have money in an account in that financial institution. With a debit card, you can spend only the amount that you have in your account. It looks just like a credit card, but instead of borrowing the money from some company that wants to charge you a ton of interest, it takes money from your own account. The obvious limitation is that you can only spend as much money as you have in that account. That is the idea! Spend less now so you can have more later!

If you are thinking of re-mortgaging your home to find the capital to pay off credit cards, it might make sense, but you need to be very careful. If you have gotten yourself in trouble with credit cards, most often (but not always) it is due to your attitude toward money, not something that the credit card company has done. You need a different way of thinking about your life now and in the future. You need to change the way you behave. Something about how you think and feel is preventing you from using control over your purchasing. If you don't fix that problem, doing a re-mortgage at a lower rate will just make your problem worse. You will be adding more debt and giving yourself the opportunity to abuse credit cards again. Change your attitude first, then:

- Destroy all credit cards but one for emergencies only, before you take on a re-mortgage debt. Remember that excessive debt is the cause of your financial difficulties. Adding another debt load even at a lower rate might not be the best choice. Get a debit card.

- Commit to paying the debt you have added to your mortgage before you make any new major purchases. Don't forget that a loan spread over a thirty-year mortgage, even at an attractive interest rate, can cost you much more than a higher rate credit card, if you keep that low rate debt for the full thirty years.

For your children, credit cards are a non-issue. Make it simple. Do not give them a credit card and do not co-sign for a credit card unless you are very, very sure they have a mature enough attitude to handle it. Start them with a debit card! If you want them to have access to a credit card for emergencies, make sure it is only used for emergencies![3]

## Spending and Saving

This book is not a get rich quick scam. We have no magic formulas for winning lottery numbers. You, however, can make a positive change in your financial future and you can make your children rich. There are financial tools that you can use that were not available in the past. But you can't use these tools unless you first save some money. To improve your finances, you will need to act.

We want you to put some of your money in savings that

will provide you with economic security. This is step one to the accumulation of significant wealth. We hope that you already have a retirement plan, a 401(k), an individual

retirement account (IRA), a 457(b), a 403(b), or some property left to you by Uncle Fred. Beyond that, we want you to save a little more. Some of that money we want you to invest in your children's future and some we want you to keep for your own future. To save more money, you will have to earn more or spend less. While we encourage you to think of ways to earn more money, we suspect it may be easier to accumulate wealth by spending a little less. Everyone has a unique financial situation, but most people in America can live a very reasonable life buying fewer things.

Our goal is to have you, and your children when they are old enough to have jobs, save 5 percent of your yearly gross income up to a maximum of $4,000 per year, or $10.96 per day.[4] If you can do that, we can show you how to make that money grow for you and grow even more for your children. And when your children understand that you are doing this for yourselves, they are more likely to do the same for themselves, and their money (because they have a longer time to invest) can become positively huge.

How are you going to save more money? We are going to ask you to spend less money. This is not easy for many, and it is very difficult for Americans in particular.

Spending less now so you will have more later is called deferred gratification, a concept you will need to teach your children and follow yourself. We want you to buy less stuff and save, then invest that money. Just as we want you to teach your children, you need to make choices. You can have more stuff now or you can have wealth and comfort later. The choice is yours.

If you think there is an obsession here with too much "stuff", you are correct. How much "stuff" do Americans have? For the fourth year in a row, Norway is ranked as having the highest standard of living, and the highest per capita income in the world. However, Norwegian homes average just over four rooms.[5]

Americans, with notably less income and a lower quality of life, have the largest homes in the world, with a new average home of 2,200 square feet.[6] Even this is not enough room to hold all the "stuff" Americans own. Having too much stuff has even created the huge self-storage industry, with hundreds of thousands of units to store stuff all across the country.

Is there a problem with this picture? Our mass media are paid for by advertisers who urge us all to buy more stuff.

There is nothing dishonest here. They want to take your money and they will give you stuff in return. We suggest that you keep your money, and invest it and get rich. *The Overspent American: Why We Want What We Don't Need* by Juliet B. Schor (Basic Books, 1998) is a scary look at today's buy, buy, buy culture. Her latest book, *Born to Buy: The Commercialized Child and the New Consumer Culture* (Scribner, 2004), paints an even scarier picture about our children's financial future. You can and should be the person in control of your own finances, not some marketing guru behind a TV ad. To do that, you need to spend less and save more—and teach your kids to do the same.

You are the driver of this financial minivan (your kids are in the back), and you need to make the decisions. We do not think that driving a vehicle with worn-out tires is an intelligent way to save money. The lives of your family and others on the road are much more important than saving the money that you need to spend on tires. However, tires can be a lot of money and you should spend the time to find a good deal rather than buy from the first place you see. Plan ahead so you can find a good deal. Planning ahead lets you take more control. If your tires die on the highway, you may have to spend money on a tow truck and pay a high price for whatever tire you can find. So, waiting too long is not a good idea. Planning ahead gives you more control and more power. Spend the time to shop around, and don't forget that if you see an advertisement for tires, the price of the tires includes the cost of that ad. Some tire re-seller who did not pay for an ad may be able to offer you a better deal.

Sometimes the very simple things are overlooked. If you

have money and buy something from a store, you give the money to the store. You do not have that money anymore. If you keep the money, you can make it grow: investing the money to make more money for yourself. But if the store has your money, you cannot make that money grow. And if you don't save, you can't invest.

*"Nick, I'm having a hard time with this. The book tells us to pay off our credit card debt, and we have hundreds of dollars that we have owed for a long time. But this book also wants us to save 5 percent for our retirement. And then it wants us to fund the retirement program where I work. But we should buy tires if we think the ones we have aren't safe. That is nuts! We can't do everything!"*

*"It's priorities, that's all. Relax, Heather; we can figure this out. Don't you get matching funds from your company in your 401(k)?*

*"They match 50 percent, up to 3 percent of my pay."*

*"That is the same as making 50 percent per year on an investment. That has got to be the top priority. Nothing will beat that rate. So we need to make sure that no matter what, we put at least 3 percent into your 401(k)."*

*"What about the credit card debt? It is not getting any smaller."*

*"Sure we want to get that debt paid off, but we are paying out about 25 percent on that and your 401(k) is giving us 50 percent. So, the 401(k) is more important. But that 401(k)*

*money is coming out of your pay now and we don't even miss the money. The credit card debt is next. How much do we owe?"*

*"We have our usual monthly charges and we have about $2,000 we owe them in addition. But I always pay off how much we spend each month. Well, I almost always do. But I guess what we owe has been getting bigger over the last year."*

While some would reach for a calculator, Nick did the math in his head. *"Damn! We are taking some bum at the credit card company out to dinner each month. They are making forty dollars per month profit off us. Every month! How long have we had that debt?"*

*"I don't know. Over a year, I think."*

*"Every month for a year. He is eating a free dinner*

*paid by us! We should rip up that card!"*

*"Hey Nick, chill out."*

*"There are times I would like to go out to dinner, but* ***we can't afford that****. But at the same time, we have been paying for dinner for some guy at the credit card company!"*
*"We can pay it off. And when we pay it off, the bum at the credit card company goes on a forced diet!"*

## Budget

A budget is an accounting tool that will let you understand, from a financial viewpoint, what is going on in an organization. Your family is a financial organization. Understanding what is happening is the first step to taking control of it. However, building a budget can become a huge black hole that sucks up ridiculous amounts of your time, so be reasonable. You need to remember it is a tool to help you, and not something you should be obsessed about. It is a tool to help you make better decisions, and your decisions are more important than the tool.

The critical advantages that a budget gives you are control and power. There are three parts to a budget: 1) money coming in, 2) money going out, and 3) your decisions that control the flow of money.

You are likely to have a good idea of where your money is coming from. You have a job, and your spouse has a job, and you have some savings, and you may have some additional income from another activity. Some of this income is likely to be steady and some is likely to be irregular. An accepted principle in most financial programs is that there is never enough income.

You need to write down the amount of income you expect every month. Your budget will change as your financial situation changes (remember, changing your financial situation is what this book is all about), so you should keep this information in a format that can change. A personal computer is a handy place to do this, but many personal accounting programs are overkill, giving you an impressive list of features that you don't need and that will only get in the way. You might want to just start with a piece of paper and a pencil (not a pen). Start simple.

You are also likely to know where some of that money is going; what bills you have to pay. Like your income, some of these costs are likely to be fixed (rent, car payments, etc.), and some will be irregular, like a credit card payment. You need to write this information down; having a budget only in your head is severely limiting. On paper, your initial budget might look like this:

**Our Monthly Budget**

| | | | |
|---|---|---|---|
| My Job | $1,000 | Rent | $1,000 |
| Spouse's Job | $2,000 | Car payment | $ 300 |
| Second Job | $ 500 | Insurance | $ 150 |
| | | Phones | $ 200 |
| | | Food | $ 700 |
| | | Cable TV | $ 50 |
| | | Gas for Cars | $ 100 |
| **TOTALS** | **$3,500** | | **$2,500** |

But you know you don't have an extra thousand dollars left over every month, so you will need to update this budget to get it closer to reality. A budget can be started in ten minutes, but you will need to work on it for weeks. For example, you may think that you know what your bills are going to be, but a check of what you really spend may show something else.

You should also assume that you will have an "extraordinary expense" several times a year. Extraordinary expenses are events that will happen but you cannot predict when. For example, your hot water heater may fail. Obviously, you will need to replace it at once; it should last for many years, but hot water heaters or cars or washing machines or whatever can fail at any time and need to be fixed when they do.

Simple short-term savings are for events like your water heater. The easiest form of simple savings is to have more money in your checking account than you are planning to spend. You might call it a buffer. The key is that you need to have this savings in place, because at some point you will need it.

One of the major dangers of credit cards is that you may have an unexpected "extraordinary expense" for which you have not saved. You may be forced to use the high interest credit card. Don't get caught in this trap. Have some money set aside, because even though you do not know what it will be, you can be sure you will get an "extraordinary expense" at some point, and you don't want to be trapped into using your credit card.

How detailed you make your budget is up to you. Once it makes sense to you and reflects reality, you should not spend hours every week updating it. As we warned you earlier, the details of a budget can create a black hole of time that masks the more important purpose of a budget: to give you control and power over how you spend, and over your financial future. When you know where you are financially, you can make an informed decision to buy or not to buy stuff.

There are budget forms that you can get for little or no cost on the Internet. See our Internet support page at www.KidsFutureUSA.org for more information on both computerized and non-computerized budget systems.

## Financial Planning

You need to have a long-term financial plan. Some planning you can do on your own, but some can be tricky. Let's start out simply.

How long do think you are going to live? Obviously, you don't know, but you need to make as highly educated a guess as you can. For example, a key influence is your family history. If your grandfather lived to 94 and your grandmother to 103, it is likely you will live a long time. If you smoke cigarettes and are two hundred pounds overweight, it is likely you will have a short life. You can research average data on the Internet, searching for "actuarial tables."[7] If you own life insurance, you can ask your agent.

What financial issues do you have now and what do you see in your future? For example:

- You want to buy a house.
- Your grandfather is going leave you a pile of money.
- Your car is about to fall apart.
- You want to take your family on vacation.
- You give 10 percent of your income to the church.
- You plan to retire by the time you are fifty or seventy.

What is your net worth? This is not that hard to figure out. It is basically what you have—cash, investments, property, and businesses—less what you owe.

Once you have collected this information, you need to create a plan for getting the things you want in the time you have, starting with the resources you now have. The first step is to prioritize your wish list. You should have many more things that you want to do with your wealth than you will have the time and money to do. That is a good thing. But you need to get real about planning. Some things are critical and some are not. The choices are yours. Do NOT try for a detailed plan because you are talking about the future and you do not know what the future will bring. But if you make and follow a plan, you may be able to take advantage of events that occur.

At this point, you will probably see that you are going to need to start saving. Congratulations! That is good news: saving is one of the keys to wealth.

Abdul Khadam[8] has been reading this book: *"Part of my interest in this is selfish. Fifty years from now, my kids will not remember if they had a used bike or a new mountain bike or no bike at all. But if I can put together a plan for them to be financially secure when they are retired and I am gone, they will know that I did something important for them. They will be able to see the difference between themselves and the others who spent all their money and will be broke for the rest of their lives. I hope that they remember that we worked with them to make their financial security happen.*

*"Some parts of this plan won't be easy. But there is even an advantage to that. It is the hard things that you remember. You remember the difficult tasks that you accomplish, not the things that you found easy. I want my kids to remember what we tried to teach them about finances. When that money provides for them in later life, they will remember me."*

## Transparency

Transparency is a term now popular in corporate accounting circles. It means that financial things are not hidden and are understandable for those who need to look at the company books. This is a constructive step, with modifications, that can work for your family.

In previous generations, one individual—the man of the house or the wise old grandmother or some other individual—would handle the finances. It may be tempting today to "let the wife handle the bills" for your family. But I urge you to make the financial decisions reasonably open so that your children can understand that everyone is actually involved in family finances. While it seems intelligent and efficient to have one family member pay the bills, we hope that the decisions about how the family money is spent is a shared task. Open means that all parties need to be involved, to the extent that is appropriate for their role and age.

Here in America, money and family finances have often been hidden secrets that were not discussed, ever. A key step to building wealth for your children is to expose them as early as is reasonable to financial decisions. They need to understand that money does not grow on trees. This is not to say that the bills should be reviewed by everyone, but that decisions as to expenditures, debts, etc. should be discussed. The key here is that children need to see that there are choices that need to be made. Their exposure to choices should be as early as possible. Obviously, no one will want family finances to be shared with all the five-year-olds in the neighborhood, and we trust in your judgment as to what to include and what to leave out at what ages.

The key point is that you need to show your children that you make *choices* about spending money, and that there are multiple issues to consider in a financial choice. You need to demonstrate to your children how to use their intelligence in making financial decisions and not just their emotions, which are too often shaped by the marketing efforts of advertisers.

## Chapter Summary

- You need to teach by doing if you expect children to believe you.
- An appropriate attitude toward money is critical for you and your children.
- You need to have some structure to your financial life.
- A budget is a tool to gain control over finances.
- Gaining control over your finances and making better decisions is the goal; the budget is just a tool toward that end.
- Debt is a powerful, useful, and very dangerous financial tool.
- You need to do some basic, long-term financial planning.
- Saving money is critical, and the best way to save money is to spend less.
- Credit cards are the most dangerous form of personal debt and cost Americans BILLIONS of dollars each year.
- Making good financial choices is a critical skill you must teach your children; to do so, you must share with them the financial choices you make in your family.

[1] http://www.bcsalliance.com/creditcard_profits.html

[2] There are many companies that will assist you with credit card debt, and some of them are honest. Our suggestion is to contact Kim Corwin (one of our Millionaire teachers), who can be reached at www.NewLeafFinancial.com. (Her photograph is in Chapter 10)

[3] In a broad sense, the creation of this book and the operation of our non-profit corporation are "faith based" initiatives. We believe in value and earning and profit and work and responsibility for the Greater Good. We think that the profits that MacDonald's and Microsoft and Fidelity Investments earn are justified by the value they offer. However, we fear that the huge profits credit card companies take may not reflect reasonable value for many consumers.

[4] This is the current maximum for people ages forty-nine and younger for investing in the Roth IRA. That amount will increase.

[5] Statistics Norway, www.ssb.no 2004 © Statistics Norway

[6] National Association of Home Builders. www.nahb.com

[7] For example, see the "Period Life Table, 2001" http://www.ssa.gov/OACT/STATS/table4c6.html 4/27/05

[8] Actually from California, Khadam has, co-incidentally, the same name as the Iraqi policeman hero that stopped, at the cost of his life, a suicide bomber trying to disrupt the first Iraqi elections.

# Chapter 5: Kids Learn Early

When children are born, a good practice in the earliest months is to give them everything they want. Feed them when they are hungry, burp them when they have gas in their tummy, change them when their diaper is wet. Hold them often and have fun with them. Absolutely the most important thing you can give your children is your time and attention. There is nothing you can buy that is as important as your time and attention.

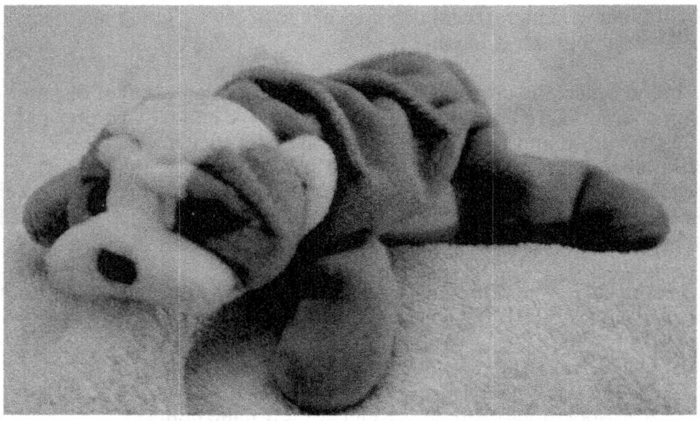

Now comes the hard part: if you take your time and attention away from your child to go buy something for your child, you may be downgrading your relationship with your child. Every year, billions and billions of dollars are spent on stuff for babies. Some of it is important. Some of it is unnecessary and wasteful. It all costs money. The important thing for the child is your time and attention, not the stuff. A rattle for a new baby will get his or her attention for a few minutes and then it is likely to be thrown away. Your baby just gave you a message, the same message this book is giving you: Your time and attention are more important to your baby than anything you can buy. Your children don't need all that stuff; they need you to save money.

What stuff do you not buy? You are the driver and you need to decide. But does your baby need five soft and cuddly toys? Lots of people may want to give your baby a soft and cuddly toy. We suggest you not buy some of those cute things. You might consider making some room in the crib for cuddly toy gifts from friends, but not buying that toy yourself, and saving your money.

It is not easy to buy less stuff, and you have lots of people working against you. There are thousands of companies in this country that want to trade their baby stuff for your hard-earned cash. Lots of sales "associates" are trying to feed their own children by selling you more stuff. Highly paid advertising executives are working hard to pay for their new yachts by working an emotional hook into the TV ads for baby stuff.

The American focus on owning stuff as the way to a better life is simply wrong. There are things that clearly can make people happy, but owning lots of physical objects is not one of them. Ironically, spending the time and effort to pay for those things often takes away from those things that may make us genuinely happy. Happiness can consistently be found in accomplishments, recognition, personal relationships, health, financial security, contributions to others, and a good marriage. Buying stuff consistently creates a flow of cash out of your pockets, which is likely to prevent financial security, which, in turn, can clearly prevent a person from being happy.

For a laugh at the truth, you might listen to what the well-known and intelligent comedian George Carlin has to say about "stuff". See www.carlinstuff.com (but beware of his extensive use of "adult" language).

Let us give you a little truth about those cute TV ads. They will show you an ad with a happy baby in a $760 crib with fourteen stuffed cuddly toys, $75 sheets, a special $60 pillow, and two mobiles. But the truth is that before the picture was taken, the baby was crying because of the chaos and strangeness of all that stuff, and is only smiling now because his mother is standing behind the photographer making funny noises. What is important to the baby is that his mother is about to pick him up and hold him and play with him. The baby understands that the mother is good and warm and soft. The baby does not understand all the things in the $760 crib. There is nothing you can buy for your child that is as important as your time and attention. We have important things to do with that money and if you don't think buying one less $20 stuffed toy makes a difference, keep reading...

# Attitude: Self-Efficacy

Creating the right attitude in your children may be the most important step you can take to make them wealthy.

Self-efficacy[1] is a belief in one's own ability to produce the necessary or desired results. This is an attitude that you must instill in your children. You want your children to be proactive in creating wealth, not expect everything to be given to them by their parents or by the government or by luck.

Your children will learn this by watching you, so be careful. When something does not go your way, do you blame someone else? True entrepreneurial individuals with high levels of self-efficacy will look at a problem or a loss as a lesson and an opportunity. Given the irritation of a flat tire, the entrepreneurial individual will start thinking about tires that don't go flat or offering roadside service or selling prepaid, one time use, emergency cell phones. The basic concept of self-efficacy is that you can control most aspects of your world.

When something goes wrong, do you complain a lot? If so, it is a sign that you have not grasped self-efficacy, and nor will the children who hear you. Complaining and blaming reveals a negative attitude; it says, "I am not in control of my life; my life controls me; the best I can do is just get by."

Such an attitude encourages waiting by the telephone for Prince Charming to call; waiting for the lottery to pick your number, waiting for the pot of gold to fall out of the sky at your feet. An extreme expression of that attitude is the "victim mentality", which breeds paranoia and conspiracy theories. If you wait for things to happen, you can only be assured that you will get old.

If you feel as if the world controls your destiny, you are probably right. But you can change that: you can take control of your life, and you can improve your world. This is the essence of self-efficacy. If you want your children to be rich, assure them that they can be rich, if they take action and personal responsibility to make it happen. Waiting will not work. They have to make it happen for themselves. Your attitudes will be the ones they are most likely to learn, so pay attention to your own outlook on life - and take responsibility for it.

Your children will have more choices and more opportunity and more financial tools than you have. As a parent working to offer them a financially secure future, you need to let them know that they are the masters of their future. We have no choices about the circumstances we are born into, but we have many choices about our future. Your children will make their own choices; they will make mistakes, but they will control their own destiny. If they can internalize this one fact, their chances for future success will be greatly enhanced.

## Choice Battlegrounds: Kitchen and Supermarket

To your children, you are a teacher. The first priority in teaching is communication. Teach your children about choices. About the time children can recognize supermarket items they want and communicate that to you, you can start to teach them the concept of choice. Obviously, the concept of choice requires an intellectual development on the part of your child. Think about it! As a baby, even before they could use language, they let you know what they wanted, and you gave it to them. Now they can communicate so much better, in language, but they can't get what they want. Big change!

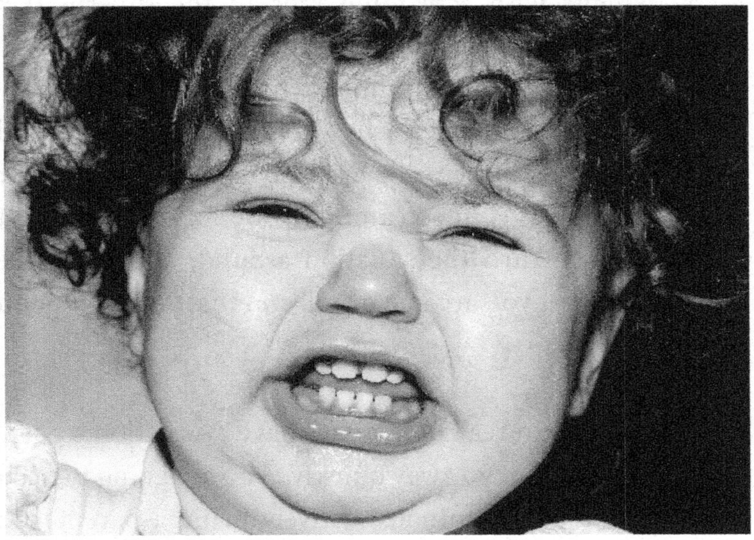

It is not reasonable to think that "choice" can be taught in a single lesson. Be patient and work on it again and again. Kids have very short spans of attention and if you cannot get the idea across in thirty seconds, give up and try again at a later time. You will have many opportunities.

## Oh No!

That same child who, as a baby, got everything (and probably more) he or she wanted has become a two-year-old and every other word out of his or her mouth is "No" or "Mine." You take that two-year-old to the supermarket and we all know what happens. Your lovely little child becomes a monster who demands items and will humiliate you with a scream loud enough to be heard three stores away if you don't do exactly what he or she wants.

Many parents with screaming kids in the supermarket become very embarrassed at their defiant and demanding children. We urge you to calm down, and know that every parent has had the same issues. You are not embarrassed because of your children; you are embarrassed by the other adults listening to your screaming children. This is a great opportunity to turn the situation around, and show the other adults that you are in control, and that you are a good parent.[2]

The first step is to realize that you have a situation to deal with, and it will not go away quickly. You are going to need to spend five or ten minutes actively being a parent and teacher. Accept that whatever you planned to do next, is now an additional ten minutes away. Change your mind and your attitude from being a shopper to being a parent. Think about it: being a parent is much more important than being a shopper. Once your attitude is straight, you can make good progress. If you can't assume the right attitude, your kids will gain control over you, and your chance to be a parent in this situation is gone. It is your choice: you can be in control or your child can be in control.

When this happens we encourage you to act quickly and firmly. Do not sink to the level of your screaming child. Above all, do not get physical; no grabbing by the arm or swatting on the butt. Try a time out. Have the child sit down on the floor, right there in the supermarket aisle, facing away from you. Then take a few steps back. If you do this well and do it early, this, like many other parenting tactics, can eliminate problems down the road. Tell the child that he or she is going to be put in time out, if the fussing doesn't stop. The first time you say this, it will have no effect, because he or she won't know what it means, but children learn quickly.

*"Learn quickly! I will never forget the day that Vera had a fit at the supermarket."* Nick Korman is talking about one of his parenting traumas. *"It was not a good situation because I had Vera and I had to go pick up her mother at work, but I had to get food for supper first. Vera is in the shopping cart basket and we are tooling around getting stuff and I gave her a piece of cheese, which she loves, at the deli counter. Then, in the checkout, she sees some kind of junk candy, says 'Mine,' and reaches out for it.*

*"The cart starts to tip over, so I grab it and yell 'No!' She falls a little in the basket and I pick her up and she goes nuts. I thought she might have been scared by the fall, but no way: it's the candy! She is twisting around in my arms and is going for the candy and yelling. Everyone turns around and looks at me and the kid is bawling her eyes out, and the*

*checkout guy is too freaked out to ring up my stuff. I never want to go through that again. How am I supposed to use this 'opportunity' to TEACH her something?"*

Heather, a wise mother, comments to Nick: *"My guess is that you were more upset than you think, and she figured that out and thought something was wrong. That may have been what the fuss was all about, she was reading you and you were upset."*

Heather offered a better example of her own parenting in the supermarket. *"She and I did do that 'Choice' thing in the supermarket. She wanted something, I think it was a plastic pinwheel. I asked her if she wanted cheese, which of course she did. This distracted her from the pinwheel, and we went over to the deli counter and the lady gave me a slice for free. I pulled off some of it and gave it to Vera, and went back to the pinwheel. When we got there we did the choice thing with the*

*rest of the cheese and the pinwheel. She went for the cheese. She got a little fussed as we went away without the pinwheel, but I think she got the idea of choice. The next time we were there, she pointed at the pinwheels, and with a big smile said, 'Cheese.'"*

## Choice is Critical

How important is the concept of choice, and does it need to be taught at an early age? You can postpone teaching the notion of choice as long as you want. However, you will pay a price for not teaching it early, and the difficulty of teaching it later can be substantial. Choice is a critical concept to understand and internalize for financial wealth. Understanding and internalizing the idea that choice is possible obviously will benefit your children in other areas of their life. When a child learns to share a toy she wants to play with, she has learned to make a choice. If you can address choice early, you may not have to hear the phrase "has difficulty sharing" from your child's day-care teachers. Choice is very, very important.

Because choice is so critical to teach, it makes sense to be proactive and prepare lessons ahead of time, and structure the environment for a lesson. Your kitchen may be a good place for this exercise. Let your child pick a dessert from several choices. Use the term "choice" multiple times so that he or she understands only one item may be selected. Remembering that you will have only about thirty seconds of attention, you need to keep it simple. Trying this multiple times will be much more beneficial than belaboring the point past your child's very short attention span. With kids, instincts often work better than dogma, so use your best judgment.

## Kids with Money

At some point, your children will start to handle money. We would encourage you to hand them the money to pay for the groceries at the supermarket, being sure that they understand that the money is your family's money. This is an excellent opportunity to establish attitudes about spending, spending limits, and choices.

The ubiquitous bank ATMs are a point of confusion for children.[3] If you are reasonably open about money, a visit to the ATM is a good opportunity to explain to a child that the money you are getting is your money and not the bank's money. The only reason you can get money out of the ATM is that you gave that bank the money to keep in a safe place for you. If you did not save the money in the bank, you would not be able to get any money out of the ATM. This is a great opportunity to work on attitudes toward wealth and savings.

## Allowance

About the time your child gets into elementary school, start him or her with an allowance. There are several critical points that should be made with an allowance. The money should be entirely their money to spend in any way they want, within legal and what you see as appropriate limits. You are strongly encouraged to set as few restrictions as possible. Clothes, school books, and other such critical items should be covered in other ways. An allowance provides the opportunity for them to learn about money. Ideally, clothes, food, housing, etc. should not be not their responsibility, and you should make it clear that spending their allowance money will not affect what you spend on them.

It is useful to start a savings plan when you start an allowance. Out of their allowance, children should put a specific amount into savings and other amounts for items you may think appropriate, such as donations to help others or to your church.

It is critical that children be allowed to make poor choices and mistakes. They should have the same rules that you have: they can change their mind about which candy they buy—until it is paid for. An excellent step is to give them advice but to point out to them that it is their allowance, and they can do whatever they think is appropriate. It is also very important that they live with their mistakes. Don't bail them out of a bad choice. Let them learn!

Their allowance should be a fixed amount that they can be sure they will get on a regular basis. Get them to mark when they get their allowance on a calendar so they (and you) can keep track. Make this accounting function be their responsibility.

They need to understand that their money is theirs to spend as they see fit, but your money or family money is different, and must be treated in a different way.

Be careful not to supplement their allowance. For example, if they have fifty cents and want a seventy-five-cent item, do not loan them the money or give them a little more so they can get the thing. Encourage them to save.

In the beginning, don't trouble them about making interest on their savings or funding college or investing; just encourage them to save.

If they want a big item that will take weeks of savings, you may consider matching their savings, like many retirement plans. Kids have a short attention span and if your child makes the effort to save over a period of time, that is a very important step (and a huge opportunity for you) and a reward is entirely appropriate. However, you need to include "fine print" that says they only get the matching funds if they meet their savings goal. Obviously, you need to explain all this when you start the matching program, not when they decide to skip the bike they wanted, to buy forty-five lollipops instead.

You should plan on and announce years in advance that your child's allowance will end at a specific point, perhaps on his or her sixteenth birthday. At that point, you should explain that he or she should be able to get a job that will provide the needed income. Note that such a discussion is a great opportunity to set a positive attitude toward jobs.

*"For Christmas a few years ago, my parents sent Nick and me and the girls to Disneyland. It was really great. Natasha was six and Vera was four. We told Natasha she had fifty dollars for the entire week and she could spend it any way she wanted. The very first day she saw a yellow "Princess Jasmine" outfit that she had seen in a movie, and that she*

*wanted. It was forty-five dollars. We agree that is very important for our kids to be able to make choices and live with the results, but we did not want to have a real problem all week. We tried to talk her out of it, because it was the only thing she would be able to buy, and it was made out of this flimsy-looking, see-through material that Nick was sure would rip right away.*

*"But that is what Natasha wanted. We compromised and said that she could buy it on our last day if she still wanted it. She did not spend another penny the entire week, and on the last day yellow "Princess Jasmine" outfit is what she bought.*

*"The real surprise of the story is that she wore that outfit for years. It was almost indestructible. I have no idea how Disney made it, but it was outstanding quality. Natasha was right, we were wrong. She got an excellent value."*

# Chapter Summary

- In raising children, nothing you can buy is as important as your time and attention.
- Buying your kids "stuff" may feel good to you, but your children may not like it at all.
- Teach your children at the earliest age possible.
- Choice is a critical concept for children to learn.
- The supermarket is a challenging place with kids, but it is a place where you can teach choices.
- Children should get allowances not connected to family chores.
- Allowances should have well-communicated parameters—the amount, how long it will last, and the choice of saving up for big purchases
- Children must be able to make their own choices and MUST be allowed to make the mistakes that will help them learn.

[1] Albert Bandura is a key author on the topic of self-efficacy.

[2] We found a good article with suggestions at http://xtramsn.co.nz/health/0,,8006-3949008,00.html 4/15/05

[3] See **Toy ATMs hit jackpot with kids** by Ann Gerhart of *The Washington Post* and posted on January 20, 2005, in the *Honolulu Advertiser.*

# Chapter 6: Middle School

## Savings

As you talk about choices and financial issues with your child, point out that not spending money now can create opportunities at a later time. Make clear that one choice they have is to save money. The concept of saving can be taught in the elementary school years, but will fade gradually as students get older. Opening a savings account is more difficult than it was fifty years ago. It is also more important than ever before that the concept of saving be easy for your children to grasp. Our recommendation is that you start with an envelope in a desk drawer. Be sure to be careful about keeping track of the money that is added. It is a useful step to have your children see you take the time and make the effort to do accounting-type functions with their money. It reinforces the importance of saving with actions as well as words.

The concept of saving and your positive reinforcement are much more important than the amount saved. If you get the attitude right at an early age, the savings and the rewards will follow.

You can take this one step further. Consider establishing financial goals for your children and rewarding them when they reach those goals. For example, give them a goal of saving ten dollars, and reward them with an additional two dollars when they reach that goal. Managing the savings yourself in your desk drawer also has the advantage of making a big event out of reaching a large goal, such as taking the money to a bank to start a formal account.

## Long- and Short-term Savings

Obviously, there are limits to how complex you can make personal finance for your child. However, at some point you will be able to split savings into long-term and short-term savings. An ideal situation might be that your child will want some stuff that you approve of, but that your child does not have the money to buy. There are a number of positive strategies that you can employ in this situation.

First, tell your child you have an idea how he or she can buy the thing, but you both need to think about it for a day. Lesson here is that an important financial decision need to be thought about overnight. This will surely not be taken well, but it will work if you follow through with the plan.

If the child has savings at that time, one option might be to let him or her take some money from savings and spend it. If you take that option, you create an opportunity to explain that short- and long-term savings are different.

If he or she does not yet have savings, use this situation to start a saving plan with the goal of buying the thing. You can make a major event out of buying the item when the goal is achieved. Going on a shopping trip for that item and that item only is an excellent opportunity to do some major parenting and enjoy your child's company. Don't give a lecture, but do point out that he or she was able to buy the item because of having a plan and a goal, and that you are proud of your child's accomplishment.

## Deferred Gratification

Learning to save is a step toward deferred gratification, but it is only part of the story, since it focuses on the deferred aspect, and has a somewhat negative connotation. Saving is taking something you CAN use and making it something you CAN'T use. Becoming a millionaire shifts the focus to gratification, and saving is a key step to becoming a millionaire.

Rather than using the imperative: "You should save your money," have your children arrive at that conclusion themselves. Focus on the goal: "Do you want to be a millionaire? You can't become a millionaire if you don't save your money." If you communicate the choice successfully, you will create some confusion and difficulty for your child. Is the ice cream cone now more important than becoming a millionaire later on? Not an easy decision, if the child is old enough to understand the choice. The difference between telling your kids what to do and presenting it as a choice for them to make may seem slight, but it is significant, and you should use every tool you can to get your ideas across. Politicians call it "spin"; others call it marketing.

Judge for yourself. Which would you prefer:

Save your money for a rainy day.

or

Become a millionaire.

Maria Rogers, a single mom who lives in Florence, Alabama, has been volunteering in the elementary school sports program. She found a good way to explain deferred gratification to fifth graders:

*"Tonja, you need to learn about making good decisions and one of the things you need to understand is a term called "deferred gratification". Those are big words that mean that you might want something right now, but it would be better to have it later. Let me give you an example:*

*"Pretend that you are on a basketball team and you are the star player and you have a really important game this afternoon."*

*"I'm ready."*

*"But someone has just given you a really big ice cream cone. And you just had three slices of pizza for lunch"*

*"Three slices? I'm stuffed"*

*"That's right. You are stuffed and you have all that ice cream in front of you.*

*"Tonja, are you ready for the hard part?"*

*"Do I get to eat the ice cream now?"*

*"Ah ha! That is the problem. What will happen to you if you eat the ice cream, and then go out and play basketball?"*

*"Oh, Coach Rogers, that would be really gross. I'd probably get sick and puke all over the place."*

*"Yes, you are absolutely right. It would be much better to play the game first and have the ice cream later. You could even have an ice cream party with your teammates. That is what deferred gratification is—waiting till a later time to use something you could have right now. I also want to point out to you that babies can't do deferred gratification; they want their food right now. But you are not a baby. You are eleven years old, and this is something you can learn to do."*

While the words are big, there are some advantages to using the concept of "deferred gratification." When you talk about saving, it is not good to focus too much on the deferral, without pointing out the eventual gratification. We are going to show you how to make that gratification huge, but you can't get the gratification without the deferral. Back in Chapter 3, we talked about how you did not need so much stuff for your child. We noted that you, also, may have wanted to get lots of stuff (shopping is fun and people are happy when you give them money), but we encouraged you to save the money. Your child will be going through the same emotional issues of wanting stuff and finding it difficult to save. Be aware of this and work with your child early to address these emotions.

## Jobs Are Good

Have you noticed that the mass media have little interest in work and jobs? TV shows cars being wrecked every hour of every day, but seldom shows cars being built or designed. Ads are always saying you should "relax and take it easy" or "get away and leave the troubles to us." Work is seen as a negative thing. The financial system in this country is dependent on work and initiative, but the message of the mass media is to "beat the system."

This is not an intentional decision on the part of the media; it is the nature of the beast. Watching people work or watching flowers grow is not nearly as exciting as winning money or being handed a bouquet of roses. The media shows us exceptional events that will catch our attention and bring them advertising dollars. Unfortunately, the cumulative effect for kids of watching many thousands of hours of TV and seeing few hours of people actually working severs their connection to the real world. You need to help your children understand how the real world works, that jobs can be very rewarding and that most millionaires earned their millions by working hard and following intelligent plans.

We are living in a nation that has created immense wealth for more people than any other country or economic system in the history of the world. While that wealth may be concentrated in the hands of a few, wealth, even great wealth, can be gained by ordinary individuals here in America. There are approximately 2,500,000 millionaires in the USA. The best way to wealth is to work, save, and invest. Naturally, there is room for improvement, and there are some problems with the system, but it is clearly one of the most powerful wealth creation systems in the world. As you may have noticed, the story that the best way to wealth is to work within the system, does not generate the kind of excitement that the mass media like. The media tend to focus on sudden wealth, such as on winners of lotteries. State governments spend over $300 million per year to encourage such games, which belittle the ethic of work and achievement and replace it with an ethic of luck.

Unfortunately, many children honestly think they can gain wealth by winning games on TV. Of course they do; that is what they see on the TV every day! Explain to your child that thousands of people bring home hundreds of thousands of dollars every year for creating and selling TV programs in this country. The so-called "winners" your children see on game shows are really just working for the really rich people that produce the TV shows and sell products with the advertisements.

As a parent you have major, powerful forces working against you, as you teach your children how the economics of the world really work. We want you and your children to get rich. We strongly encourage you to talk with your children at as early an age as possible about how to create and protect wealth. There are millions of people in this country with a net worth of over $1 million. A few of them won their million in a lottery, and fewer still might win their million on TV each year. But the hundreds, and thousands, and tens of thousands, and hundreds of thousands and millions of other American millionaires get their millions by working, saving, and investing. This is an important message you need to send to your kids, because they see a different story on TV.

We want your children to work, enjoy work, and be rewarded by work. There are a number of things you can point out that are not obvious to kids who spend too much time watching TV:

- Doing a job well makes you feel good.
- A job is a great place to meet interesting people.
- People respect a person who does a good job.
- The good jobs are not the easy ones, but the challenging ones help you grow.
- The financial benefits of a job go way past take-home pay.
- Jobs are a great opportunity to learn new things.
- Jobs help you define who you are.
- Glamorous jobs and titles are often the ones that pay

non-famous people the least.

- Jobs will often pay for additional education.
- Jobs are an opportunity to help other people.

Kids live in a very small world. They are not likely to read newspapers or pay attention to the news. They are more geared toward entertainment than financial events. The good news is that the truth about how this country works is exciting: it allows ordinary individuals to thrive. Kids can make the system work for them, but you need to tell them how! TV will not teach them the way things actually do work, but you can!

## Chapter Summary

• Establish a pattern for your children of saving, and reward them when they reach saving goals.

• Deferred gratification is another key concept for children to learn as early as possible.

• Jobs are good and are much more than just a way to make money.

• Mass media show kids that making money is winning a game or lottery. Tell them the truth.

# Chapter 7:
# The Magic of Mathematics

You have now set the attitude and education platform to build serious money for your child. Now let us introduce you to some of your partners: mathematics and the Taxpayer Relief Act of 1997.

## First, the bad news

Saving alone will not create wealth. Your children cannot put enough money in the cookie jar to gain economic security. No way. Not even close. Do the math. This example is simple because the answer is so obvious.

- They earn $50,000 per year.
- They save 5 percent, which is $2,500.
- They spend $32,500.
- Taxes take the rest.

- Their income goes up, but inflation takes it away.
- They work for fifty years and retire.
- After fifty years, they have saved $125,000.
- They'll get the equivalent of about $1,000 per month from Social Security.
- Their overall cost of living stays about the same.
- They are broke in less than seven years.
- They have twenty more years to live and perhaps $12,000 of yearly income: poverty.

You can adjust this scenario to fit what you guess will be your children's situation, but don't bother; the result will be about the same. For example, if you increase their income, you can assume they will live longer and senior citizen expenses will be higher. If you think they can save more, that 5 percent figure is at least four times the national average now. You can figure in inflation, which means you will start to see their dollar income increase but the value of their savings go down at the same rate. If you think they will increase their income by gaining skills and getting better jobs, that is great. But they will also increase their expenses at the same time. These adjustments are unimportant as the numbers are totally overwhelming.

For 97 percent of the people in this country, it will be impossible to put money away in a sock drawer and ever have economic security. Savings alone will not make it.

## Now, the good news

You know that you can earn income by putting savings in investments that generate a profit. The bad news is that every time you earn a little income, you will usually have to pay taxes on that income.

Let us introduce you to the **really good news**. The Taxpayer Relief Act of 1997 has within it a tax shelter designed to help you save. A tax shelter is a legal program that shelters you from paying taxes. You can put your money in a tax shelter and you will have to pay little or, in this case, NO taxes on that money. It is totally legal because the federal government wants to encourage you to invest your money for retirement. This tax shelter is called the Roth IRA[1]. IRA stands for Individual Retirement Account. The program was conceived by the late Senator William Roth Jr. (R-Del.).

The government thinks that you can save your own money and make your own decisions about how that money will be invested and later spent. In many parts of Europe, you do not have these choices, but you can count on the government taking care of you. In the United States, we do thing a little

differently, and you are the person in charge. The only thing is that you need to take action, and you had better not make any big mistakes!

We hope you have heard of the Roth IRA. If you are younger than 50, it is something you should consider for yourself. You MUST consider this program for your children as soon as you can (probably when they reach eighteen).[2]

Because it is a law, and because it is about taxes, the Taxpayer Relief Act is long and complex. There are certain income requirements, investment limits, withdraw requirements and more. For example, if your child is making more than $95,000 per year, there are restrictions on how much he or she can put in a Roth IRA. (If they are making that much at age eighteen, I suspect they could find financial advisers to assist them in a savings program.)

There is a different IRA program that has been around for much longer, which allows you to invest pre-tax income, but it will be taxed when you decide to use the money. This may have been right for you at one time, but your children will likely do much better with the Roth IRA. You can put money you earn and have paid taxes on into an investment covered by a Roth IRA, and you may not have to pay taxes on it, EVER. If the Roth IRA sheltered money is put in an interest-paying investment or in the stock market, and it makes lots of money, it is all TAX FREE. You will never have to pay taxes on that money while it grows or when you take it out and spend it, as long as you keep the money in a Roth IRA until age 59 ½.

You need to understand that a Roth IRA is a legal system that shelters the funds within it from taxes, and is not, in itself, an investment. (Note that you are reading a brief summary of a complex legal document, and are encouraged to find professional resources if you have specific questions.)

The Roth IRA is like a truck that protects its cargo from rain and snow. The money you put in the truck is protected from additional taxes, even if the amount of money increases. Like a truck driver, you can earn money with the Roth IRA, if you drive the truck around and do some work. If the Roth IRA money, like a truck's cargo, just sits in the parking lot, you will not make any money. You will need to invest that Roth IRA money, which will require effort, like driving the truck to different destinations. You pick the investments/destinations. If you learn and are careful, you can make a lot of money. When you make that money, the Roth IRA truck legally protects the money from taxes, as long as you leave it there until you are over 59 years old. No taxes taken out means more money for you!

The Roth IRA was signed into law in July 1998 and was amended in 2001. Because this is a relatively new program, many adults have not invested in it, and a number of people do not know about it at all. Some people are talking about it now, but in forty years everyone will be talking about it, because it will be making them rich!

[As this is being written, the President's Advisory Panel on Federal Tax Reform (lead by Connie Mack III and John Breaux) is considering a number of constructive changes to the Roth IRA. There are some smart people in Washington, and we hope that you will see an even better Roth IRA soon.]

## The Miracle

The next step is to explain "compound interest," a mathematical and financial phenomenon that is often called a miracle, and that Albert Einstein is said to have called the eighth wonder of the world. It may seem dull, and it will involve spending time looking at a chart of numbers. However, the reward of accumulating compound interest over a number of years is attractive. If you use the number of years your children have left to live, the reward is very attractive. When you then combine it with a Roth IRA, the result is **huge** — in fact, it is a financial miracle.

Assume your child has a job making $20,000 per year, and at the end of the first year has saved $1,000. If that $1,000 is put in a Roth IRA, and then is invested in something that pays 10 percent interest,[3] a year of interest will be $100; at the end of the first year, that account will be worth $1,100. We want your children to keep adding money to their Roth IRA, but for now let us follow just this initial $1,000.

In the second year, that $1,100 ($1,000 of savings, plus the $100 of interest) will earn an additional $110 for a total of $1,210. In the third year, the interest (tax free in a Roth IRA) adds $121, which gives a total of $1,331.

In eight years, the value of that original $1,000 has more than doubled to $2,144. And every year it gets better and better. In another seven years it has more than doubled again. In another ten years, that single investment of $1000 is now worth over $10,000. After fifty years, that single investment of $1,000 is worth over $100,000! This is called the miracle of compound interest.

After fifty years, you are making almost $10,000 in interest every year, all on a single investment of $1,000.

Unfortunately, just as compound interest will add to your investment, inflation will reduce the value of your investment. The good news is that compound interest can give far, far more than inflation is likely to take away.

On the next two pages you will find a chart that gives you this example. Look at how the interest grows and grows!

*ROI is total return: interest, dividends, sales profits, etc.

| YEAR | Child Has | Child Saves | ROI* | TOTAL |
|---|---|---|---|---|
| 1 | $0 | $1,000 | $0 | $1,000 |
| 2 | $1,000 | $0 | $100 | $1,100 |
| 3 | $1,100 | $0 | $110 | $1,210 |
| 4 | $1,210 | $0 | $121 | $1,331 |
| 5 | $1,331 | $0 | $133 | $1,464 |
| 6 | $1,464 | $0 | $146 | $1,611 |
| 7 | $1,611 | $0 | $161 | $1,772 |
| 8 | $1,772 | $0 | $177 | $1,949 |
| 9 | $1,949 | $0 | $195 | $2,144 |
| 10 | $2,144 | $0 | $214 | $2,358 |
| 11 | $2,358 | $0 | $236 | $2,594 |
| 12 | $2,594 | $0 | $259 | $2,853 |
| 13 | $2,853 | $0 | $285 | $3,138 |
| 14 | $3,138 | $0 | $314 | $3,452 |
| 15 | $3,452 | $0 | $345 | $3,797 |
| 16 | $3,797 | $0 | $380 | $4,177 |
| 17 | $4,177 | $0 | $418 | $4,595 |
| 18 | $4,595 | $0 | $459 | $5,054 |
| 19 | $5,054 | $0 | $505 | $5,560 |
| 20 | $5,560 | $0 | $556 | $6,116 |
| 21 | $6,116 | $0 | $612 | $6,727 |
| 22 | $6,727 | $0 | $673 | $7,400 |
| 23 | $7,400 | $0 | $740 | $8,140 |
| 24 | $8,140 | $0 | $814 | $8,954 |
| 25 | $8,954 | $0 | $895 | $9,850 |

| YEAR | Child Has | Child Saves | ROI | TOTAL |
|---|---|---|---|---|
| 26 | $9,850 | $0 | $985 | $10,835 |
| 27 | $10,835 | $0 | $1,083 | $11,918 |
| 28 | $11,918 | $0 | $1,192 | $13,110 |
| 29 | $13,110 | $0 | $1,311 | $14,421 |
| 30 | $14,421 | $0 | $1,442 | $15,863 |
| 31 | $15,863 | $0 | $1,586 | $17,449 |
| 32 | $17,449 | $0 | $1,745 | $19,194 |
| 33 | $19,194 | $0 | $1,919 | $21,114 |
| 34 | $21,114 | $0 | $2,111 | $23,225 |
| 35 | $23,225 | $0 | $2,323 | $25,548 |
| 36 | $25,548 | $0 | $2,555 | $28,102 |
| 37 | $28,102 | $0 | $2,810 | $30,913 |
| 38 | $30,913 | $0 | $3,091 | $34,004 |
| 39 | $34,004 | $0 | $3,400 | $37,404 |
| 40 | $37,404 | $0 | $3,740 | $41,145 |
| 41 | $41,145 | $0 | $4,114 | $45,259 |
| 42 | $45,259 | $0 | $4,526 | $49,785 |
| 43 | $49,785 | $0 | $4,979 | $54,764 |
| 44 | $54,764 | $0 | $5,476 | $60,240 |
| 45 | $60,240 | $0 | $6,024 | $66,264 |
| 46 | $66,264 | $0 | $6,626 | $72,890 |
| 47 | $72,890 | $0 | $7,289 | $80,180 |
| 48 | $80,180 | $0 | $8,018 | $88,197 |
| 49 | $88,197 | $0 | $8,820 | $97,017 |
| 50 | $97,017 | $0 | $9,702 | $106,719 |

In the real world, this is not as simple as it looks above. It is historically and statistically impossible for you to get a steady 10 percent return for ten or more years. (Please see chapter 11.) Time and investing are the real keys, as long as you take advantage of the tax benefits of the Roth IRA. The Roth IRA may help you with your own financial situation, but if you can get your children to start saving their money and investing with a Roth IRA, it can have a huge impact on their futures. Because they have more time than you do, the power of time and interest-compounding has a greater effect on their savings.

The next step to economic security is obvious: add to the Roth IRA every year. You need to understand that the gain you get from that first $1,000 will never be matched by your future investments. With every year that goes by, you will have less return on your investment. The key to the huge return from this plan is time. The longer the investment is working for you, the more money you are likely to earn. That is why the plan is aimed at your children. A Roth IRA can make a profitable return for you, but for your kids, with the amount of time they have, the result can be HUGE.

Obviously, we want you to have your children put away as much money as they can every year. We think that they should save an amount equal to 5 percent of their gross income in a Roth IRA every year. You should remember that time is the key, so the longer that time can work on their savings, the greater the impact will be. This means that you need to start the program as early as possible. DO NOT skip the first years, as they are the most important. When you add $1,000 or more every year, at the end of fifty years, you could have over $1,000,000 (One Million Dollars!) in tax-free savings.

Let us repeat again so it is clear. You gradually put $50,000 into a Roth IRA; with a 10 percent return, after fifty years, $1,000,000 comes out, tax-free! Or you might not take it out, and let it sit and earn you $100,000 per year in interest. A guaranteed income of $100,000 per year. Do you understand why this is called the miracle of compound interest?

| YEAR | Child Has | Child Saves | ROI* | TOTAL |
|---|---|---|---|---|
| 1 | $0 | $1,000 | $0 | $1,000 |
| 2 | $1,000 | $1,000 | $100 | $2,100 |
| 3 | $2,100 | $1,000 | $210 | $3,310 |
| 4 | $3,310 | $1,000 | $331 | $4,641 |
| 5 | $4,641 | $1,000 | $464 | $6,105 |
| 6 | $6,105 | $1,000 | $611 | $7,716 |
| 7 | $7,716 | $1,000 | $772 | $9,487 |
| 8 | $9,487 | $1,000 | $949 | $11,436 |
| 9 | $11,436 | $1,000 | $1,144 | $13,579 |
| 10 | $13,579 | $1,000 | $1,358 | $15,937 |
| 11 | $15,937 | $1,000 | $1,594 | $18,531 |
| 12 | $18,531 | $1,000 | $1,853 | $21,384 |
| 13 | $21,384 | $1,000 | $2,138 | $24,523 |
| 14 | $24,523 | $1,000 | $2,452 | $27,975 |
| 15 | $27,975 | $1,000 | $2,797 | $31,772 |
| 16 | $31,772 | $1,000 | $3,177 | $35,950 |
| 17 | $35,950 | $1,000 | $3,595 | $40,545 |
| 18 | $40,545 | $1,000 | $4,054 | $45,599 |
| 19 | $45,599 | $1,000 | $4,560 | $51,159 |
| 20 | $51,159 | $1,000 | $5,116 | $57,275 |
| 21 | $57,275 | $1,000 | $5,727 | $64,002 |
| 22 | $64,002 | $1,000 | $6,400 | $71,403 |
| 23 | $71,403 | $1,000 | $7,140 | $79,543 |
| 24 | $79,543 | $1,000 | $7,954 | $88,497 |
| 25 | $88,497 | $1,000 | $8,850 | $98,347 |

*ROI is total return: interest, dividends, sales profits, etc.

| YEAR | Child Has | Child Saves | ROI | TOTAL |
|---|---|---|---|---|
| 26 | $98,347 | $1,000 | $9,835 | $109,182 |
| 27 | $109,182 | $1,000 | $10,918 | $121,100 |
| 28 | $121,100 | $1,000 | $12,110 | $134,210 |
| 29 | $134,210 | $1,000 | $13,421 | $148,631 |
| 30 | $148,631 | $1,000 | $14,863 | $164,494 |
| 31 | $164,494 | $1,000 | $16,449 | $181,943 |
| 32 | $181,943 | $1,000 | $18,194 | $201,138 |
| 33 | $201,138 | $1,000 | $20,114 | $222,252 |
| 34 | $222,252 | $1,000 | $22,225 | $245,477 |
| 35 | $245,477 | $1,000 | $24,548 | $271,024 |
| 36 | $271,024 | $1,000 | $27,102 | $299,127 |
| 37 | $299,127 | $1,000 | $29,913 | $330,039 |
| 38 | $330,039 | $1,000 | $33,004 | $364,043 |
| 39 | $364,043 | $1,000 | $36,404 | $401,448 |
| 40 | $401,448 | $1,000 | $40,145 | $442,593 |
| 41 | $442,593 | $1,000 | $44,259 | $487,852 |
| 42 | $487,852 | $1,000 | $48,785 | $537,637 |
| 43 | $537,637 | $1,000 | $53,764 | $592,401 |
| 44 | $592,401 | $1,000 | $59,240 | $652,641 |
| 45 | $652,641 | $1,000 | $65,264 | $718,905 |
| 46 | $718,905 | $1,000 | $71,890 | $791,795 |
| 47 | $791,795 | $1,000 | $79,180 | $871,975 |
| 48 | $871,975 | $1,000 | $87,197 | $960,172 |
| 49 | $960,172 | $1,000 | $96,017 | $1,057,190 |
| 50 | $1,057,190 | $1,000 | $105,719 | $1,163,909 |

In Chapter 3, we spoke about you not buying another $20 stuffed toy, and suggested that there were better things you could do with that money. Perhaps now you are starting to get the idea. Take that $20 and save it. If you put it in a bank account; it will slowly grow, but you will have to pay taxes on it. After eighteen years, it might be worth about $40. That is not much money, but you now know about some powerful financial tools that can make your money grow dramatically. Your children's money will have even more time to grow. Unfortunately you can not directly put your savings into your child's Roth IRA, but they can...

## Support Your Child's Roth IRA with Your Savings

The Roth IRA requires that the money invested be earned in the year it is invested, by the person who is investing it. This means that your child must earn and pay taxes on the amount invested and that money needs to be earned in the year it is invested. This is one of the great parts of the Roth IRA, in that it requires earned income. Your children need to find jobs, keep jobs, and contribute to society. This is a very good thing.

This requirement, however, does restrict you from just adding money directly to your children's Roth IRA as a gift. But we have a plan. You have already gotten your child excited about getting a job and saving money. Your child needs to earn money in his or her eighteenth year, which can be put in his or her Roth IRA. Most eighteen-year-old kids do not make much money and often find it difficult to save. So if you saved some money for this child and offered to *match the amount he or she earned* with those savings, he or she would be able to put all their earned and taxed income into the Roth IRA legally. You are likely to have been giving your child an allowance for many years. You can give up to $11,000[4] to each of your children, every year, without facing any gift taxes yourself, and without your children owing income taxes on the gifts. Look at this example.

Since your baby Chris was born, you have been saving money for his Roth IRA. You haven't had much money, but you have been able to save $5 per week. You know it will be really needed many, many years down the road. Chris is now eighteen; he works at a restaurant, and earns $5,400 per year, which is, after taxes, about $5,100. For eighteen years, you have saved $5 per week for Chris, which is a total of $4,680. Chris opens a Roth IRA. The maximum amount he can put in that account is currently $4,000. You give him $3,000 from your savings and he then takes $4,000 from his $5,100 income and puts that $4,000 of earned, taxed money in the Roth IRA. Everything is legal, because your child will be careful to see that only his earned income is put in his Roth IRA, not the money you saved for him. He now has $4,000 in his Roth IRA, but has been able to spend up to $4,100 for himself. And after fifty years, that $4,000 alone could amount to well over $500,000.

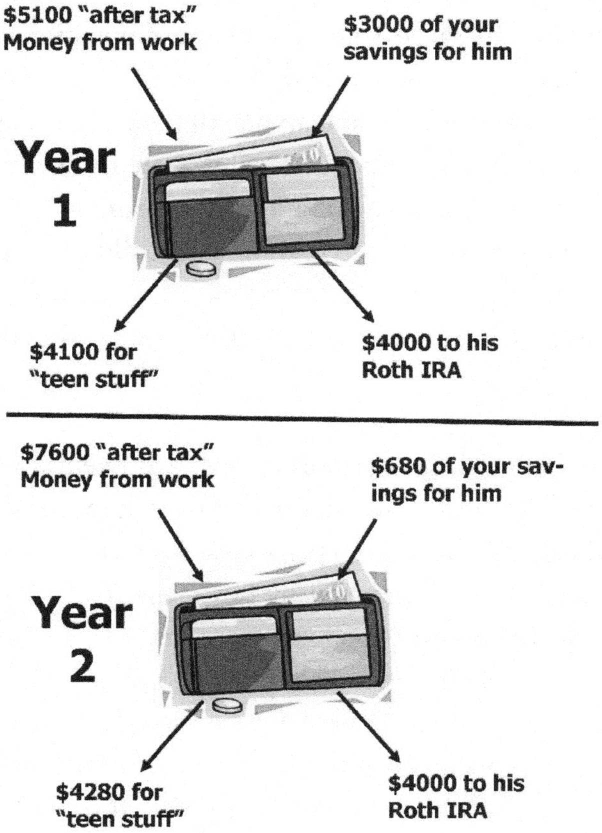


The next year you can give him the rest of the savings you have for him, and you can expect he will be able to earn more income. Make sure he adds enough to enter the maximum permitted from his own cash. The year after that, he will need to use only his own money for the Roth IRA, but he is likely to have increased his income, as he has more work experience.

Think about this again. You only saved $5 per week, but by following this program, you may have given him as much as $500,000: FIVE HUNDRED THOUSAND DOLLARS. And you have given it to him at a point when he will really need it, and it is tax free. In addition, you will have shown him the results of making a plan and following through on that plan, shaping his attitudes.

Remember the money from that single stuffed toy you didn't buy? It is now in his Roth IRA. If he can earn 10 percent on that money, in fifty years, that $40 will be worth $4,269. He did not get another stuffed toy as a child, but he got $4,269 in tax-free cash when he really needed it and could appreciate it. Save a little and win BIG.

You know your children will need to have substantial wealth for the second half of their adult life. The problem is how to get them that money. Our program has two steps that you take at the same time.

1) You save every penny you can for your children and have them open a Roth IRA as soon as they can. You match their earned and taxed income with your savings up to the maximum permitted in a Roth IRA, but require (because it is the law) they put only their own money in the Roth IRA. You do this as long as your savings for them exist, maximizing their early IRA investment.

2) At the same time, you educate your children and help grow positive attitudes about their ability to control their own financial future, make choices, defer gratification, enjoy work, and save. Their attitudes will last much longer

than your savings for them, or your direct supervision and guidance.

*"Heather! These numbers are incredible, and I know they are true. It is not magic, but the effect of time on money that is invested is humongous. Time is the key. Saving will be useful for us, but the real deal is for our kids. They have the time, and we now have a plan to make the future totally awesome for them."*

*"I actually think that the numbers will be a little different, but the result will be even better. The government is pushing up the retirement age now. People are learning to live healthier lives, getting exercise forever, and starting to eat better. By the time our kids retire, the age of retirement will be way past seventy. That will give them even more time to let their money in the Roth IRA grow. But what will inflation... Heather, I've got to use the computer."*

Nick was back in about half an hour. *"Heather, even with inflation and putting in only $1,000 per year, in sixty years that will give them an income of $40,000 in today's dollars per year. That is an incredible amount of money! We put in $1,000 per year for sixty years and every year, it is easier to put in that $1,000. So that is 60,000 bucks in. At the end of sixty years, the kids will be able to have $40,000 of today's dollars in interest, every year, year after year after year!"*

*He paused for a second, then continued:*
*"But all my figures are based on a straight line projection."*

*"What does that mean?"* asked Heather.

*"It means I am using the same amount each year for savings. And that is my point. In the real world, those numbers will change. We help build up savings in the early years of the Roth IRA, by helping to support our daughter's lifestyle. She puts her money in a Roth IRA, but she is free to spend the same amount, which we supply from our own savings."*

*"Wait a minute, that is silly. The government will never be able to figure out whose money it is, but it will be easy for them to track the amount of earnings the kids make. So you can only put in an amount equal to their take-home pay.*

*"But our savings will run out quickly and the amount they put into the Roth IRA may go down for a bit. But later when they start to make real money, they will be able to put in more. So using a straight line is not accurate."*

Heather was excited by Nick's enthusiasm, but was a little confused by all the financial talk. She saw a logical issue:

*"Accurate? How can you be accurate when we are talking about our kids getting jobs and how much they will be saving when they are still sleeping in our room half the time?"*

Nick answered: *"They will grow up. If we can give them a headstart with our savings, get them to save some of their money, shelter it in a Roth IRA, and investments, they will be set for at least half of their lives."*

## Chapter Summary

- Savings alone cannot give your children enough to live reasonably. Not even close.
- Investing your savings can make them grow faster.
- The Roth IRA will let your invested savings grow without paying any taxes.
- The Roth IRA is only a "vehicle" for investments and is not an investment in itself.
- Compound interest is a mathematical miracle that lets money grow to huge amounts over time.
- Time is the key for compound interest, and your children have much more time than you do.
- Saving for your children can help their retirement programs, but must be done carefully to avoid conflict with the Roth IRA law.

[1] You are welcome to look at www.Roth IRA.com, but it may be more detailed than you want.
[2] This should not be considered tax advice and we advise you to speak with your accountant or financial planner if you have any tax questions.
[3] Does 10 percent sound unlikely? See Chapter 11.
[4] This is the amount may increase in the future. These statements are not tax advice. Please check with your accountant if you have any questions.

# Chapter 8: Saving Money

Now that you understand what a huge financial opportunity you have, how are you going to save enough to make it happen? If you can't save, then you can't invest, and the tax savings of the Roth IRA won't matter because you won't have any money. Everything starts with saving money. There are lots of other things that are involved, but unless you can save some money to start with, we can't help you get rich. Our suggestion, outlined above, is that you save money for your children when they are very small, and use that savings to support them as they add earned and taxed money to the Roth IRA. Our example in the last chapter saved $5 per week, which grew to over a half million dollars.

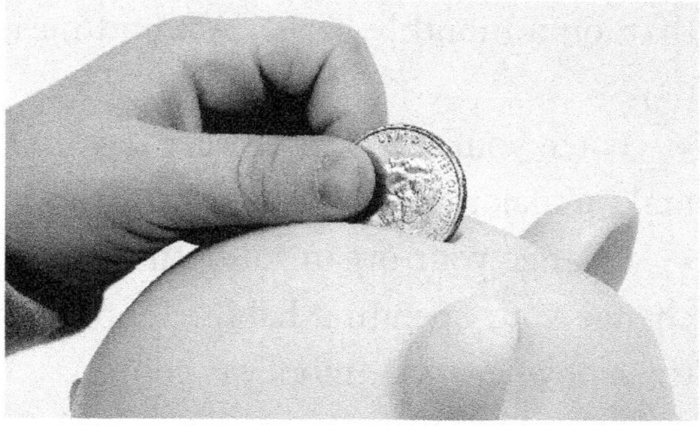

Saving is easy for anyone who has been saving for a long time, and it is hard for anyone who has not been saving. If you have never saved money in the past, you can save money in the future, but you will have to change your habits. Saving money is a learned habit, and anyone can do it. Changing habits is not easy, but there are a number of steps you can take that will greatly help you.

- Accept that saving money will mean buying fewer things.
- Accept that saving money may not be easy and setbacks will happen.
- Remember that you can change your behavior with a focused effort in a fixed amount of time.
- Understand that saving money on a daily basis is easier than on a monthly basis. Act and measure success every day.
- Force yourself to save every day for thirty days. It can make a major change in your future.
- Change your organization habits at the same time you change your spending habits. For example, start keeping track of where your money is going.
- Be realistic about change; don't attempt to do too much.
- Keep records! Do some analysis. How much have you been spending and saving? Compare that to how much you save once you make a real effort.
- Identify success. (You must keep records to be able to identify success.) If you have never saved before and you save a dollar, that is a success!
- Set goals and reward yourself when you reach a goal. Make the goal reasonable, like $1 per day for a week.
- Set up a family support structure and get your kids to assist. A lot of family building can be gained by working together on a shared goal.

An easy way to start saving is to make one decision on a single day. At some point you are going to buy something – something that you want, but that you don't necessarily need. Don't buy it. Save that money instead. If you can do that once, you can do it again. Saving is a learned skill and you can learn it.

Let's put things in perspective. The maximum amount you can put in a Roth IRA is, as of this writing, $4,000 per year. That is $10.96 per day. There are many people in this country who cannot save that much money. Unfortunately, too many people in this country waste more than that every day. We suggest saving an amount equal to 5 percent of your income. Five percent is far more than most Americans save today, but much less than Americans saved in the 1950s and 1960's, long before the Roth IRA existed.

*Maria Rogers has a job with the government that pays little, but the cost of living in Florence, Alabama is very low. If she invested 5 percent of her income, she would have to do without about $1,600 per year. "When I got out of the divorce, things were a mess. I had to move a couple of times, and I'm still trying to bring up a teenager. Talk about giving your kids the right attitude! A lot of the time we can hardly have a civil conversation! She already has all the 'attitudes' she'll ever need, and they ain't the right ones! She is working about ten hours a week in a pizza place, but she spends every penny. I don't think I can get her to start to save at this point, but I know she is going to be in real trouble if she doesn't. Even the idea of having a lot of money doesn't work for her, because she doesn't think she can do it. She lives for the next twenty-four hours. When she is twenty-five, things will be different, and then she will start to think about her future. I would love to have a nest egg for her about that time.*

*"Sure I want to help my kids have a reasonable life, but there*

*is no way I can come up with 5 percent of my take-home to pay for an investment. And what would happen if that investment lost money?*

*"I have been tempted to forget the whole thing, but this program is almost like FREE MONEY! It takes a long time, but my mom is still goin' strong at ninety-two. So my plan is to just try to save what I can and when I get to, like $500, I will see if she has that much take-home income for that year and we will get it started.*

*"I wish there was some way of keeping it out of her hands until she was twenty-five or maybe fifty-five..."*

## Adjusting to Your Financial World

Far too many people in this country, like Maria, live from paycheck to paycheck. They think it is almost impossible to save anything, much less the huge amount they will need for retirement. Often, these people are from families who have lived this way for generations. Many of these people are middle income families, but they wanted to get that boat, you know, the one that sits in their yard. The credit card was there, and they made the wrong choice. They suffer from continual family stress over financial issues and can never seem to get ahead.

The problem for them is in their mind. They need to give up some things today to make tomorrow better. The plan we have outlined will work only if they can change their attitude and start to save. Buy a used car; don't get that boat; do the lawn yourself. (Your doctor might think that is a great idea.) Once you get into it, you can accumulate substantial savings and then put those savings into good, tax-sheltered investments. It will not happen by magic and it will take some work. This is America, and that is how things here have worked for hundreds of years. Work hard and take advantage of the opportunities around you. The issue is making the right choice and acting on that decision.

For the many people who are below the middle income world, this program can have an even greater effect. If you really have no money, and millions of Americans don't, it is likely that your parents and their parents before them were in the same situation Our program is the opportunity to break that cycle of poverty. Savings at this economic level is much harder than it is for many middle income families who just have to make a few hard choices. Sometimes the money just is not there.

You will recall the example earlier of the mother who saved just $5 per week. If that is possible, you too can create significant wealth for your children. But with next to no money, it will take longer. If $5 per week is all you can do, you will be able to make an impact on the second half of your children's adult lives, but not enough to make them rich. However, if you take the steps outlined here, they will have much more money in their lives and will have learned the value of saving, investing, and using a Roth IRA. They will then have the opportunity to make their children, or grandchildren, really rich. If you are one of the American families that worries about finding enough money to buy food, this program can break the cycle of poverty, but it will be your grandchildren who will become rich. Here again it is parenting that will make the difference. By setting an example with the right attitude toward money, you can pass on to your children a way of life that leads to prosperity for them and for their children.

The process is the same, the results will be the same, but if you have very, very little that you can save or invest, it will take longer. The key to this program is time. Even with very, very little money, you can create true wealth for future generations.

At the other end of the economic scale, where the income is high, some people have found this program to be helpful with additional issues. No one knows when they will die, and no one wants to run out of money in their last years. Still, there is a desire to leave something for the children. If you can get $25,000 into a Roth IRA during the first five or six years after it becomes available to your child (generally, but not always, at age eighteen), you will have left them as much as $2 million after fifty years. Factoring in inflation at 3 percent, that account will have a tax-free value of almost $600,000 in today's dollars. If this does not sound like enough money, we are only counting on your initial $25,000, and your children would have the option to continue to fund their IRA and increase their growing fortune. So if you can afford it and can find a way to legally get those funds into your children's accounts, you need not worry about what you will leave them when you die.[1] You can then eliminate the "What do we leave the kids" issue from your future planning. You also have the assurance that their financial future is unlikely to be impacted by an untimely death or dramatic change in personal finance. Once the money is in an IRA, it is much safer than in a future plan or your personal checking account.

Following is a chart that shows earnings from investments, where $25,000 is put in as early as possible and no further contributions are made. The reason to look at this chart if you don't happen to have $25,000 is to see the power that tax-free TIME gives this investment. Twenty-five thousand dollars in and more than two million dollars out, tax free!

| YEAR | Child Has | Child Saves | ROI* | TOTAL |
|---|---|---|---|---|
| 1 | $0 | $4,000 | $0 | $4,000 |
| 2 | $4,000 | $4,000 | $400 | $8,400 |
| 3 | $8,400 | $4,000 | $840 | $13,240 |
| 4 | $13,240 | $5,000 | $1,324 | $19,564 |
| 5 | $19,564 | $5,000 | $1,956 | $26,520 |
| 6 | $26,520 | $3,000 | $2,652 | $32,172 |
| 7 | $32,172 | $0 | $3,217 | $35,390 |
| 8 | $35,390 | $0 | $3,539 | $38,929 |
| 9 | $38,929 | $0 | $3,893 | $42,822 |
| 10 | $42,822 | $0 | $4,282 | $47,104 |
| 11 | $47,104 | $0 | $4,710 | $51,814 |
| 12 | $51,814 | $0 | $5,181 | $56,995 |
| 13 | $56,995 | $0 | $5,700 | $62,695 |
| 14 | $62,695 | $0 | $6,269 | $68,964 |
| 15 | $68,964 | $0 | $6,896 | $75,861 |
| 16 | $75,861 | $0 | $7,586 | $83,447 |
| 17 | $83,447 | $0 | $8,345 | $91,792 |
| 18 | $91,792 | $0 | $9,179 | $100,971 |
| 19 | $100,971 | $0 | $10,097 | $111,068 |
| 20 | $111,068 | $0 | $11,107 | $122,175 |
| 21 | $122,175 | $0 | $12,217 | $134,392 |
| 22 | $134,392 | $0 | $13,439 | $147,831 |
| 23 | $147,831 | $0 | $14,783 | $162,615 |
| 24 | $162,615 | $0 | $16,261 | $178,876 |
| 25 | $178,876 | $0 | $17,888 | $196,764 |

*ROI is total return: interest, dividends, sales profits, etc.

| YEAR | Child Has | Child Saves | ROI | TOTAL |
|---|---|---|---|---|
| 26 | $196,764 | $0 | $19,676 | $216,440 |
| 27 | $216,440 | $0 | $21,644 | $238,084 |
| 28 | $238,084 | $0 | $23,808 | $261,893 |
| 29 | $261,893 | $0 | $26,189 | $288,082 |
| 30 | $288,082 | $0 | $28,808 | $316,890 |
| 31 | $316,890 | $0 | $31,689 | $348,579 |
| 32 | $348,579 | $0 | $34,858 | $383,437 |
| 33 | $383,437 | $0 | $38,344 | $421,781 |
| 34 | $421,781 | $0 | $42,178 | $463,959 |
| 35 | $463,959 | $0 | $46,396 | $510,354 |
| 36 | $510,354 | $0 | $51,035 | $561,390 |
| 37 | $561,390 | $0 | $56,139 | $617,529 |
| 38 | $617,529 | $0 | $61,753 | $679,282 |
| 39 | $679,282 | $0 | $67,928 | $747,210 |
| 40 | $747,210 | $0 | $74,721 | $821,931 |
| 41 | $821,931 | $0 | $82,193 | $904,124 |
| 42 | $904,124 | $0 | $90,412 | $994,536 |
| 43 | $994,536 | $0 | $99,454 | $1,093,990 |
| 44 | $1,093,990 | $0 | $109,399 | $1,203,389 |
| 45 | $1,203,389 | $0 | $120,339 | $1,323,728 |
| 46 | $1,323,728 | $0 | $132,373 | $1,456,101 |
| 47 | $1,456,101 | $0 | $145,610 | $1,601,711 |
| 48 | $1,601,711 | $0 | $160,171 | $1,761,882 |
| 49 | $1,761,882 | $0 | $176,188 | $1,938,070 |
| **50** | $1,938,070 | $0 | $193,807 | $2,131,877 |

## Spending Money

The first key to personal economic security is attitude. Americans have more stuff and generate more waste than any other country in the world, by far. You don't need all that stuff. Look around you. You are likely to see things that you spent money on just go unused and gather dust. Having money in the bank can also make you happy, and it does not require dusting and cannot be broken by kids running through the house. And having happy kids running through the house is a good thing, perhaps a lot more important than owning stuff or even having financial security.

Being sure that you are not going to starve when you are in your later years can make a great difference to how well you sleep when you are in your fifties and sixties. Make yourself feel good and make your life simpler: don't buy so much stuff and save your money. More stuff is not better.

## The Guilt of Marginal Income

These are not easy issues to deal with in your own life. If you have a small income, but you have a TV and glance through magazines, you may think your four-year-old baby needs to have more plastic toys. You want to give him or her everything that you never had. Stop! What you really want for your child are not more plastic toys, but a chance for a better life and a better life for his or her children.

# Mass Media and Your Children's Future

There are major forces working against you. America is the ultimate consumer culture. One of our great economic strengths is in sales and marketing and consumer culture. Unfortunately, this is a great strength that benefits those who are selling and advertising, but it is a major threat to most consumers -- the rest of us. Most American kids see much more advertising on TV than is constructive for them. Obviously, the ads they see are intended to take their money away and replace it with stuff. So the ads tell them that they need new stuff and everyone else has new stuff and they will be happy if they get new stuff by giving their money to other people.

The content of many programs also pushes kids into thinking that stuff is important to have. It is easier to display stuff than to explain ideas. Guns are easier to show than freedom. Sex is easier to show than marriage. Police are easier to show than the law. Counting votes is easier to show than showing leadership. The important things are mostly not shown or discussed because they are harder to do and may not be as entertaining. It is not a conspiracy against consumers; it is worse — it is the nature of electronic media. You as a parent need to understand this issue and educate your children about values and the importance of things that do not show easily on TV.

We would suggest, as one step, buying fewer things, but buying better things. I buy fancy soap. It costs $15 a bar, but it lasts many months. And it is not more stuff, because I am going to have a bar of soap no matter what. It is a luxury that, in the long run, costs little more than the low-cost competitors. I get one good thing and it replaces getting six lower-cost things.

There are two subjects here: you and your children. Because your children have had less time to form behavior patterns, it should be easier for your children than for you to change spending habits. But it may not be easy for them. Kids are kids and have a very short view of their future. Often it is difficult to get a child to plan as far forward as the coming weekend, so it may be hard to get them to think about his or her life in fifty years. This is a key reason that we urge you to begin attitude education as early as you can. Explain to your children that, if they save and invest, they can be millionaires, because, as we have shown, it is true.

You pay bills every month, we hope. Your children will also eventually pay bills every month. Once they are old enough to be earning money and having bills that need to be paid, teach them to pay themselves first. Take an amount equal to 5 percent of their gross earnings and set it aside to compensate them for their contributions to a Roth IRA, and then pay the other bills. If you start to save a little here and a little there on a daily basis, you will find that there is more money at the end of the month.

Get your children to help you save money. Kids want to be millionaires. This program can help them become millionaires. They can't become millionaires unless they save. So when you are at the shoe store and they want $175 sneakers just like those of the latest superstar basketball player, ask them if they would like to be rich instead. Buy $90 sneakers and an ice cream, and save the rest for their IRA. You could even bargain with them, so that they don't buy as much stuff. You commit to taking the money they

thereby save, and keeping it for them, until they can start their own Roth IRA.

One thing that you will have to deal with is that, when your children become teenagers, they are likely to be under great emotional pressure to be social conformists. While you know that savings will make all the difference in the world for them when they are older, it is likely to be a losing argument when they are thirteen. If this situation does occur, don't bother with the obvious logical arguments. The issue for them is an emotional one, and you will need to find an emotional answer for them. This will be a challenge; you will have to find something that makes sense to them to help keep them on the path.

One tool that you can use is the current fad of wealth. From *Lifestyles of the Rich and Famous* to *Who Wants to be a Millionaire?*, the TV culture is making wealth an attractive goal. If they want to be rich for half their adult lives, you have a plan. If they want to get fabulously rich tomorrow, let them play with the idea, and consider it a victory. At least they are thinking about the issue. At a later time you will perhaps be able to have a more rational talk. The key that you impress on them early is that they have to accept personal responsibility for shaping the future they want to have.

## Chapter Summary

- Everything starts with saving money.
- Saving money is a learned habit; anyone can do it.
- Many small steps can help you learn to save.
- Really working at it for thirty days can make a big difference.
- Keep records so you can measure and celebrate success.
- Attitude is the key: you must use emotional as well as logical appeals to have your children work within the plan.

[1] Everyone has a unique situation and you should consult your lawyer and accountant prior to taking any action.

# Chapter 9: Investing

When investing, we suggest you think of the world directly around you, as well as the stocks and bonds of Wall Street. Investing is a way of using your money to make a profit. You can invest by purchasing seeds for your garden and sell the plants, making a profit. That would be investing locally.

You can also invest by buying stocks in a corporation in another state or country. That would be investing globally, since a person anywhere on the globe can make this type of investment. With a local investment you are using your money directly to make a profit. With a global investment, you are letting someone else use your money to make a profit. There are advantages to both types of investing.

A Roth IRA cannot be used to shelter most local investments, but local investments may have advantages that outweigh the disadvantage of not having a Roth IRA to shelter the profits. Investing using a Roth IRA can make you rich later on in life; investing locally can make you rich sooner. Both are good ideas.

Real estate is perhaps the most common type of local investment. This is the house you live in, not the get-rich-quick scams. For example, back in the 1980s I made $100,000 profit in less than four years on a home that was purchased with a 10 percent down payment. That money was not covered by a Roth IRA, but making a profit on your home can also be a tax shelter. The untaxed profits from the sale of that house were rolled into my next house, and I don't expect ever to pay taxes on that profit.

Many people have found that they make local investments that do well (doing well is making a good profit, which often happens when you sell an investment), and then move those profits to tax-sheltered, global type investments.

Investing is a complex endeavor with substantial risks and substantial opportunities. You need to be careful. We think that you yourself should learn about investing. You are likely to be investing for most of the rest of your life. However, as investing is not simple, we suggest you get advice from others who know about the risks and benefits of investing. **Money is too important not to seek and use good advice.** Good advice could come from a local farmer or a grocery store manager, if you were going to invest in seeds and a garden. If you are thinking of investing in local real estate, you should talk to local real estate professionals and property managers.[1] If you don't know what a property manager is, you have some research to do before you make global investment in real estate.

If you want to consider doing some corporate investing (stocks and bonds), there are hundreds of investing books on the shelves of your local bookstore, magazines, shows on TV and the radio, and financial professionals from many firms eager to assist you. Most Americans have investments of one type or another, and investing may be the best way to gaining substantial personal wealth. If you want to build real wealth, you have no choice: You must invest. At the same time you must understand that investing involves risk.

You should use your own common sense as well as the advice of professionals. Remember: if it sounds too good to be true, it is likely to be too good to be true. If you hear a story about an investment that is guaranteed to give you 50 percent profit in one year, it is safe to assume that it is just that -- a "story." Investing in "stories" may give you memories, but will almost never give you profits. With a Roth IRA, you have a powerful financial tool that does not require you to make a 50 percent profit in one year, or even 20 percent. The Millionaire program is a sure thing, but it requires time and savings. It does require that you not LOSE your invested savings on a high-risk "story." We urge you to be conservative with money by investing in a Roth IRA. Investments that give dividends may be more useful than one that returns profits in capital gains. If you don't understand the difference between dividends and capital gains, you need to learn more about investing.

Since your investing will be done over a long period of time, it is best to start with conservative investments and some advice and education. After a decade or so, when you have accumulated enough funds to diversify, you might consider taking a small portion of those investments and managing them yourself. These rules apply to yourself and to your children. Being "good with money" is a learned skill; you can learn, and your children can learn. Just learn before you act!

We cannot give specific advice to you on your investments. Legally, we are not even permitted to give you specific advice. However, we want you to get rich, and should you have a specific question, you are welcome to contact us at advice@KidsFutureUSA.com; we will put you in touch with a financial professional who may be able to assist you. The personal financial industry is highly regulated, very profitable, and rapidly growing. Many personal finance consultants are eager to assist you. As in any industry, most are honest, reliable, and intelligent professionals, but some are not.

You should certainly consider investing in yourself and learning about investing. Get books and magazines, read them, go to seminars that are offered by personal financial consultants, listen to the financial news on the radio or TV. Empower yourself. The financial professionals you consider enlisting to assist you in getting started will be paid by you in one way or another, and you can eliminate much of that expense by learning about the world of investing yourself. Again, you need to exercise caution when investing.

Merrill Lynch, Fidelity Investments, Schwab, Vanguard, and many, other financial companies are eager to help you establish a Roth IRA. You can guess why: They believe they will make a profit from assisting you.

## Fees and Charges

You need to be careful about fees and charges, which is why

we suggest learning about investing and eventually taking direct control over your own investing. For example, your financial adviser may charge you $35 to set up a Roth IRA, and then charge you 2 percent for investing in a stock mutual fund, which then has a 3 percent management fee of its own. This would be over 6 percent in fees on a $3,000 investment. That makes it very difficult for you to see any profit, and a profit is what we are looking for!

There are limits to the type of investments you can make with a Roth IRA. The easiest investments you can make are likely to be stocks, bonds, mutual funds, index funds, and REITs. Let us look at each of these areas.

## Stocks

Owning stock means you are a part owner of a company. If you buy one share of Microsoft, you own 1/10,794,693,000 of the company, or about one-eleven billionth of the company. (After the many stock splits, there are about 11 billion shares that are owned by people around the world.) If Microsoft makes a profit, and if the management thinks it is in the best interest of the company to give some of that money to the stockholders

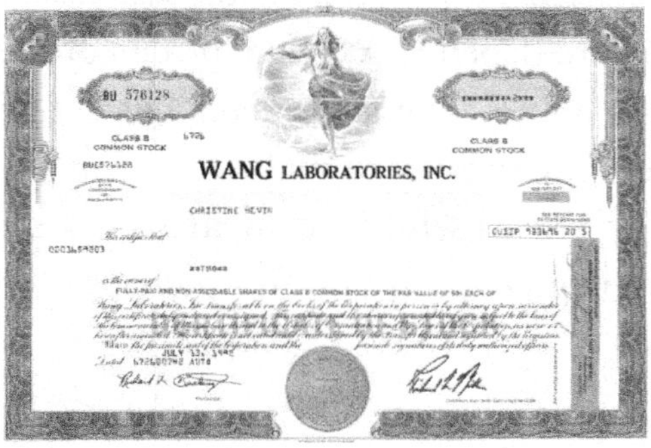


(which would include almost all the employees and

the founders), you would get one-eleven billionth of that dividend. Microsoft is a very large and well-run company, but it is not likely to create huge profits for you, should you decide to invest in it. Many people would suggest that money invested in Microsoft is relatively safe. Microsoft is not likely to go out of business soon.

However, size and reputation alone are not always good indicators of profit or safety. There was once a very large company in the energy business called Enron that generated great profits for their investors and was highly regarded by many financial analysts. While that sounds great, there were crooks in the management of the company and it went bankrupt, costing investors millions and millions of dollars. The disaster also wiped out the savings of a number of Enron employees who had not diversified their retirement portfolio. Size and the image created by a public relations department are not always good indicators of good or safe investments. Investing has risk, and stocks have more risk than other types of investment!

Some stocks provide dividends, a return of some of the profits to stock holders. These dividends can not be forecasted well (unlike bonds) as they are dependent on the profits of the company. Other stocks do not offer a dividend, but put all their profits back into the company to make the company grow. You then may be able to sell that company stock for more than you paid for it, giving you a profit—perhaps even a very large profit.

## Bonds

Bonds are debt instruments. When you own a bond, the company whose bond you own owes you the money you have invested; the company offers a preset interest rate for you, and promises to pay that money back. You do not own any part of the company, so if the company does very well, you will not make any more money than the interest it promised. Bonds, in general, are safer than stocks, but the value of bonds will move up and down. Some bonds are very safe (nothing is safer than United States government bonds, but they pay little) and some bonds paying higher interest are riskier. One advantage of bonds is that they will pay a pre-determined amount of interest. You know in advance how much interest you will get.

## Mutual Funds

Mutual funds are a collection of different stocks, spreading the risk over a number of companies. Mutual funds are very popular and have returned good results over the years. If you owned stock in Enron in the late 1990s, you might have thought you were in great financial shape. But if you still owned that stock a few years later, you were in bad shape. If, however, you owned a mutual fund that had Enron stock and forty other stocks, you would NOT have lost all your money when Enron went bust. Mutual funds are a safer choice than owning a single stock.

One key additional advantage of a mutual fund is that it is managed by investment professionals, and they may make better stock purchases than you will. The danger is that they reasonably charge a fee for the management of that fund, and many mutual funds do not do much better than the overall average of the stock market. These funds will charge their fee, whether the mutual fund goes up or down. Some of the better mutual fund companies base their fees on the amount of profit they return to their investors. There are mutual fund managers who have made millions and millions of dollars for their investors, and no one minds paying those managers a fee. But some managers do not do well and you have to pay the fee anyway. Did we suggest that investing is not simple?

## Index Funds

Index funds are like mutual funds, except they are all the stocks in a given area. You do not get the advantage of an expert picking the best stocks, and you do not have to pay for management expertise. Fees for index funds are generally very low, and their performance has been often better than high fee mutual funds. As an example, the often-quoted Dow Jones Industrial Average is made of only thirty of the very largest companies in the United States. A Dow Jones index fund would own an equal amount of each of those thirty companies, would be very easy to manage, and charge very low fees, if any. **Spiders** and **ETFs** are similar to index funds but let you focus a bit more on specific sections of the market. Invest in yourself and learn about investing.

## REITs

REITs are Real Estate Investment Trusts that own mostly commercial real estate, like malls, or the large buildings you see in any downtown skyline. They pay a dividend, but unlike a bond, the amount they pay is dictated by their success in the marketplace.

A REIT's value may also change depending on the market for commercial real estate. REITs are relatively new compared to stocks and bonds, but have a good track record at providing an attractive rate of returns. They are normally taxed at a high rate, so having them in a Roth IRA lets you avoid those taxes and get the full benefit of the income they produce.

## Chapter Summary

- Investing can be done locally and globally and there are advantages to both.
- Investing is complex with major risks and opportunities.
- Professional advice is suggested until you learn about investing for yourself.
- If it sounds too good to be true, it is likely to be too good to be true.
- Many companies and individuals want to help you invest, and they all expect to be paid by you for their assistance.
- The object of investing is to make a profit; if the fees and charges for investing are too high, you will not make any profit.
- There are many different types of local and global investments. Real estate is a very common type of local investment.
- Stocks are part-ownership of a company.
- Bonds are the debt of a company and tend to be less risky.
- Mutual funds are organizations that own a large number of different stocks or bonds. They tend to be more stable than owning most individual stocks.
- REITs, index funds, Spiders and ETFs are other types of global investments.

# Chapter 10: Financial Professionals

Personal finance consultants, investment professionals, and retirement planners are in a highly regulated industry—for good reasons. You will be giving them a lot of your money and basing a lot of your future on their success. If they make a mistake, you are the one who is likely to pay for it. They are a bit like our earlier discussion of debt: they are helpful, useful, powerful, and potentially dangerous.

We suggest that you use these financial professionals, but carefully, just like debt. In the long run, it is important for you to learn as much as you can about how to create and preserve your wealth, and a financial professional is a good place to start.

The good news is that you need to save before you invest, and while you are in a saving mode, you can take the time to learn a bit yourself about investing. It is easy, perhaps even too easy, to get financial advice. You can start with the Internet, a bookstore, calls to investment organizations, etc. Be sure to get advice from multiple sources with different points of view. Much of that advice may be conflicting and that should give you an opportunity to learn.

The biggest issue for most financial professionals is sales—that is, getting more people to invest money with them. The personal finance business has often been said to be more about managing clients than managing their money. When you meet a financial professional, remember he or she is a salesperson.

Financial professionals need to get paid. They intend to be well paid. Some ways they are paid are obvious: they give you a bill. However, many times the way they get paid is hidden. You don't get somethin' for nothin.' Most financial professionals get a commission on investing your money. Sometimes they get paid multiple times for doing the same transaction. You can guess who is paying them. You are!

Many financial professionals reasonably have a minimum requirement for the amount of funds you have to invest. If you only have $1,000, they are not going to spend any time helping you. They have a business to run and a family to feed, and they cannot afford to spend a lot of time with you unless they can get paid.

It is in your best interest to be respectful of your financial professional's time. Once you have established a relationship, if you need to talk to him or her, go directly to the point and get your answer and move on. We also suggest telling other people about your financial adviser, if you think the adviser is doing a good job for you, or if you think he or she is not. Remember, your financial adviser is only one source of financial information. We strongly encourage you to empower yourself by learning more about investing, and finding multiple sources of information to validate any investment decision you make.

While most investment professionals will make a commission off your investments, there are a number of investment professionals who will work with you for an hourly or flat fee. You should carefully consider this option. While they are likely to charge you hundreds of dollars to just meet with them, they will be able to provide you with an action plan for investing that will likely save you a great deal of money over the years. Working with their plan, you may be able to invest through a low-cost investment house with minimal charges, and learn more about the industry while your funds earn income. Over the years, this can save you a great deal of money.

The stock market is exciting and people gain and lose millions of dollars every day. It can be intoxicating, and it is easy to make bad choices. Follow the advice of someone you trust. As a "qualified investor" with a successful thirty-year track record, I do not make any major investment without first checking with several sources, including brokers I know who will not make a commission on the sale.

Money is too important not to seek and use good advice. Finding the right financial professional is a very important choice; I suggest looking for gray hair and years in the industry. Unfortunately, the good ones tend to cost more, but your future is on the line. When you select a financial professional to assist you, do it in a professional way. Get multiple offers, and once you make a decision, give that individual a reasonable time to perform. You cannot invest without having situations where you lose money. It will happen. Every investor has lost some money in the stock market, but the hundreds of thousands of people who invested with financial professionals like Peter Lynch of Fidelity or Warren Buffet of Berkshire Hathaway have made millions of dollars in profits over the years.

Retirement planning is a slightly different area of investing. There are some important financial issues specific to retirement funds. You again need to be very careful, as it is easy to be talked into having a plan set up "just for you" that will cost a bunch of money (sometimes hidden and sometimes up front), but will be mostly useless.

The classic retirement sales question is "How much do you think you will need in retirement?" This sounds like an important question and it can be flattering, as it is a financial professional asking you what you think about your future. Unfortunately, the question is hogwash! The answer for all of us, unless the issue is <u>when</u> to retire, is the same: "As much as we can get!"

We encourage people who are just starting out in the world of investing to find and use good advice. However, investing is very important, and you should be selective about whom you choose to work with. In the long run, you should empower yourself by learning more about investing.

## Chapter Summary

- Personal finance consultants are in a highly regulated industry—for good reasons.
- If your finance consultant/investor makes a mistake with your money, you lose and the consultant generally does not.
- While all financial professionals expect to earn money from you, it may be to your advantage to pay a well-known individual an hourly rate (which will be high) and have him or her design a plan for you that will avoid hidden fees and costs.
- Retirement planning is a specialized area of financial consulting that deals with specific issues. We suggest finding a retirement specialist when the time is right for you.
- Money is too important to not seek and use good advice.

# Chapter 11: Issues & Answers

## Inflation

The value of money changes over time. A dollar today is worth more than a dollar next year. This is called inflation and, in moderation, is actually a good thing. As long as you understand how it works, and include it in your financial plans, it should not be a problem.

The rate of inflation changes continually, and is measured on a monthly basis. While the Federal Reserve Board makes a major effort to manage the rate of inflation, it is something the board can only influence, and not something that it can command. Three percent is considered a reasonable number to use for inflation, but note the following historical rates:

| Inflation | Rates |
|---|---|
| Mar-33 | **-10.00%** (negative!!!) |
| Feb-47 | 19.67% |
| Jan-65 | 0.97% |
| Mar-80 | 14.76% |
| 1994-2004 **Average** | 2.70% |

Look at these examples of the long-term effect of inflation.

A nice-looking 1926 Ford car sold for $580.

A current Ford 500 today starts at $23,445.

Men's fancy leather shoes sold for $5 or $6 in 1911, but today that same company's fancy men's shoes are now $78.99.

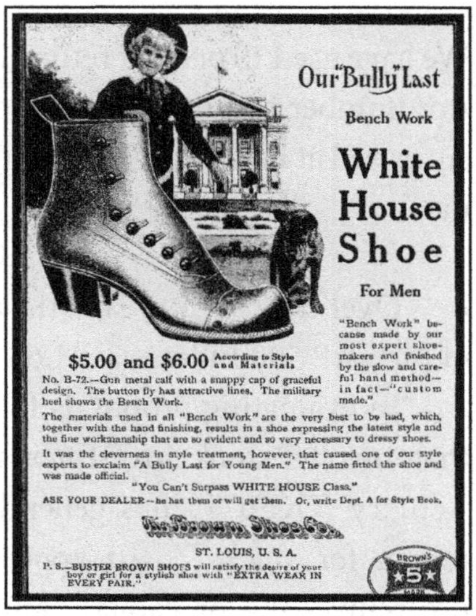


So the value of your money changes and the $1 million you have planned for your retirement will have a value much lower when it is time for your retirement. This means that it is even more important to take action for your children NOW so that they will have enough wealth to have a comfortable retirement.

If inflation increases, it

can weaken your investments, but the answer is obvious. You will need to save more money now. As of this writing, the maximum amount you can invest using a Roth IRA is $4,000 per year. $10.96 per day. Our suggestion is to consider investing 5 percent of your income for your retirement.

At the start this will be difficult, but you will adapt. When that money is invested, you will see it grow and you will know that you made the right choice. As time goes on, your children will be earning more money because they will gain more skills and experience, and because of inflation. As they earn more money, it will be easier for them to add more money to their Roth IRA. The key again is to get that money invested **as soon as you can.**

## A 10 Percent Return?

We have used 10 percent return in our examples. We picked this number because it is easy to work with. You would be surprised at how many different figures you can get for this data:

- "Over the past 50 years, the average annual total return of the S&P 500 Index was 11.65 percent."[1]
- "In evaluating proposals for reforming Social Security that involve stock investments, the Office of the Chief Actuary (OCACT) has generally used a 7.0 percent real return for stocks."[2] [It appears that OCACT does not use reinvesting or capital gains in its definition of "real

return."]

- "For the 78 years ending December 2003, the S&P 500 index returned an average of 10.4 percent per year including reinvesting dividends."[3]

| Market Returns (S&P500) | |
|---|---|
| 2004 | 10.86 |
| 2003 | 28.67 |
| 2002 | -22.10 |
| 2001 | -11.86 |
| 2000 | -9.10 |
| 1999 | 21.06 |
| 1998 | 28.57 |
| 1997 | 33.34 |
| 1996 | 22.96 |
| 1995 | 37.57 |
| **Average** | **14.00** |

Our research suggests that the 10.4 percent return most accurately reflects the returns an individual would have received over the past seventy-eight years. However, this is an average, and the investing world is very, very different from year to year. For example, the S&P 500 was up over 30 percent in 1995, **up** over 20 percent in 1999, **down** almost 10 percent in 2000, and **down** over 20 percent in 2002. It is statistically impossible that you could get a 10 percent return year after year. The market will go up and the market will go down. When you invest, you take risks, and you need to understand those risks. Past performance cannot guarantee future results, either up or down.

How you invest your Roth IRA or how you suggest your child invest his/her Roth IRA, is a complex issue. In general, you can assume that the greater the opportunity for growth, the greater opportunity for loss. Some investments are risk-free, like United States government bonds. But they pay so little that there will not be enough return to create personal wealth, even after fifty years of saving. Some investments have high risk and may give you dramatic profits but can also lose value, perhaps even all their value. Please read the section on investing, empower yourself with more investing information, and consider consulting an investment professional.

## Saving for College

Saving for college is a great American tradition, and educational institutions of higher learning are among the most successful and rewarding American businesses. They are rewarding for those who attend as students and those who are members of the faculty. There are also thousands of people in this country who are making a comfortable living helping other people save money for college. Most people think that college is important for the economic future of their children.

While college can be highly rewarding on a personal level, it may not be as financially useful as some would believe. The intellectual value of a college degree is important. However, from a purely financial point of view, the program described in this book is very likely to bring a greater **financial** reward than college. We apologize in advance to those who find such a suggestion to be politically incorrect. Perhaps the marked increases in the cost for college for many years, combined with the power of the financial tools outlined in this book, are finally overwhelming the financial advantage college once offered. Just look at the math: The out-of-pocket cost for four or more years of college education, plus years paying off education loans, can be assumed to prevent investing in a Roth IRA for the first ten years of potential funding.[4] The cost of that lack of early investment is roughly $3,400,000 after fifty years of tax-free investing. The difference between college graduate income and high school graduate income, according to government data, is less than half of that amount.

Unfortunately, it appears that what was thought to be the financial advantage of college education may no longer justify the financial cost. Please do not shoot the messenger. We are aware that this may be considered a radical attack on a cherished belief, but the mathematics are quite clear.

We again stress that the value of a college education can be measured in many ways other than money. The quality of an individual's life is not dictated by money. Note in the foreword to this book that the first person thanked is a college professor and that the book is dedicated to a math teacher. However, if you are planning to send your children to college so they can have careers that will provide them substantial wealth in their adult and later years, STOP. You need to re-read this book and rethink your planning. You may want to use the support tools offered in Chapter 13. Today there is a more effective and more secure way to find economic security than college.

We also firmly believe that early education is more critical than later education, and that if you do a good job educating your children early in life, later education will take care of itself. There are millions and millions of dollars of financial support available for promising students to attend college. The issue is to see that your child is a promising student early, knows how to work hard, and has the mental discipline to succeed in the competitive world of college. These are major tasks that largely do not involve money. They involve parenting skills, which are usually much more important than money.

## Government Limitations

Our financial program is designed to instill an attitude that encourages saving. Our "hook" is that we can make almost any child a millionaire by the end of the first half of his or her adult life with simple investments in a Roth IRA started as early as possible. Now that we have established a value for savings, we would encourage savings that have wider utility and more flexibility than a Roth IRA.

There are many restrictions to the Roth IRA. For example, you cannot take profits out of a Roth IRA prior to age 59 ½ without paying a penalty. Even more important, the type of investing you can do with a Roth IRA is severely limited. College can be looked at as an investment, perhaps a better intellectual one than a financial one, but an investment nonetheless. You cannot use a Roth IRA to fund college. The house or plot of land next door to where you live could be an excellent investment, but it would be difficult to use IRA funds to purchase that land. An 18 wheeler or a retail store or a partnership or technical degrees or a CNC lathe or a fleet of lawn mowers might all be good investments, but very difficult to fund with a Roth IRA.

Taking advantage of these investment opportunities takes money, and the best way to get that money is to save. There are limits to how much you can save in a Roth IRA, and you should consider those limits to be an encouragement to find additional, more flexible savings programs.

## Politics

The Roth IRA is a law passed by the United States government. We hope there will be other laws passed by the government that may offer even more advantages to the individual investor. The issues we have presented are well known to financial professionals and many people continue working to find better solutions. There have been attempts to create a new type of savings accounts with many advantages, but these programs might have a negative impact on some very powerful financial industries. There have been plans suggested that would change the Social Security program to include more flexible (and therefore more risky) options.[5] You should educate yourself as to the best programs available.

We all share the same country and our lives are all financially intertwined. If I can improve the financial future of your children, it will improve the financial future of my children. My editor noted that my passion on this subject shows in this book. It is the passion of a financial realist that has found a way to a better life and a Greater Good for us all.

There are powerful financial tools we can all use to improve our own lives, and most certainly the lives of our children. Our plan is straightforward and simple.

1) Put a financial program in place that will give your children a huge head start on serious wealth.

2) Educate your children so they will be able to carry on the financial program you have started.

Please let us know if this book has helped you, and how else we may be able to work together. Send email to Readers@KidsFutureUSA.org We often speak on this subject and may be able to speak to groups or institutions you are involved with. With your permission, we may be able to share your experience with others via our web site. Explaining how this system works is not enough to make it happen. Attitude is the key. The issues are not rational, but emotional. Sharing your experience with others may inspire them to take action.

[1] AIM Investments, AIM Highlights, "Stocks or Bonds?" SVB-HLT-1 1/04
[2] Peter A. Diamond, Social Security Bulletin . Vol. 63, No. 2, 2000, p38
[3] Ibbotson Associates, a financial research firm at 225 North Michigan Avenue, Chicago, IL 60601 http://www.ibbotson.com
[4] Higher education debt averages (2002) range from $21,200 for bachelor degrees at private four-year colleges to $91,700 for law and medical degrees, according to the 2002 National Student Loan Survey by Dr. Sandy Baum and Marie O'Malley, Nellie Mae, 50 Braintree Hill Park, Braintree, MA 02184.
[5] As this is being written, there is a great deal of activity concerning potential changes to Social Security, such as the implementation of lifetime savings accounts or retirement savings accounts or other types of savings programs. If you understand the principals of the Roth IRA (investments grow without taxes and can be collected without taxes), you know what to hope for in future programs.

# Index

## I



## R



## S



## T

# Support

You will find additional support and information at:

**www.KidsFutureUSA.org**

One key tool is a spreadsheet like the one described in Chapter 7 that you can alter to fit **your specific financial situation.** This tool was built using Microsoft Excel software and we make no claims as to the utility, operation, or accuracy of the program. Having made all the disclaimers, we will point out that it is FREE.

Do not forget that numbers on a computer are not the same thing as money in the bank. These are tools for planning and in no way can suggest what the future will bring. Past historical information is not a guarantee of any specific future activity.

We will also provide support systems so that you can communicate with others, including the author, registered financial consultants and others involved with Education for Economic Security, Inc., an educational, nonprofit corporation.

If you do not have access to the Internet, you are welcome to contact us at

EES, Inc.
42 Beverly Hill Drive,
Shrewsbury MA 01545

Made in the USA
Monee, IL
05 November 2026

67381747R00083